HERE, THERE AND EVERYWHERE

Here, There and Everywhere

Space in Canadian and Israeli Drama

Shimon Levy

sussex
ACADEMIC
PRESS

First published 1996 by

SUSSEX ACADEMIC PRESS
18 Chichester Place
Brighton BN2 1FF, United Kingdom

Distributed in the United States by
International Specialized Book Services, Inc.
5804 N.E. Hassalo St.
Portland, Oregon 97213-3644
USA

British Library Cataloguing in Publication Data
A CIP catalogue record for this book is available from the British Library.

ISBN 1–898723 16 8

Copy-edited and typeset in 10 on 12 Palatino
by Grahame & Grahame Editorial, Brighton, East Sussex
Printed and bound in Great Britain

To Joy

Contents

Preface

This book is based on the experience in Canadian theatre and drama that I was fortunate enough to acquire during my university years at McGill, from 1973 to 1980. At that time I was studying Samuel Beckett's work in English and French, while he himself was living his chosen exile in Paris. I also taught Hebrew drama, while the drama itself "happened" in Israel. I came to realize, in retrospect, that the geographical distance from the objects of my interest had created a necessary perspective, a degree of objectivity, that was to prove helpful again later, when this book was written. The physical distance involved in comparing Canadian with Israeli notions of space, from my Israeli space as well as point of view, also gave birth to the key-term *Offstage*, as an attempt, among the other benefits that it offered, to create a bridge between the dramatic spaces of two so different countries. While Canadian space is often experienced and described as fearsomely open, Israeli space is closed and besieged in an equally anxiety-fostering way.

Comparisons are often an attempt to engage with a less intelligible phenomenon on the basis of the relative security of a better-understood "similar" phenomenon. This study too, based on greater familiarity with the Israeli side of the equation, is, predominantly, a suggestion: to use a highly theatrical criterion as a common denominator for a dialogue between certain aspects of Canadian and Israeli drama. It may perhaps serve as a tentative criterion, in dealing with the relatively unexplored realm of comparative drama.

Acknowledgements

This publication is based on research which was supported by a grant of the Israel Association for Canadian Studies. The IACS encourages research on Canadian topics carried out by Israeli and Canadian scholars. As part of its policy to expand the knowledge in Canadian Studies, the IACS participated in the cost of publishing this book.

Introduction

Dwarfed by the majesty and immensity of their surroundings, Canadians are often accused of their "propensity for general disengagement"[1] and "emotional understimulation."[2] "You're Canadian – you're modesty itself," says a character in a Canadian play. Israelis, on the other hand, are characterized, to quote a recent opinion which is fair common local public property, as "charming, aggressive, over familiar and painfully cynical."[3] Being energetic, over-touchy, intensively involved and sometimes even frenetically creative, many Israelis often yearn for something like the prairies and vast distances of Canada, seen as a mental image rather than a geographic location, an odd compensation for the serenity lacking in their own lives.

Israel too has conquered for itself a space in many people's minds, as "part of our imaginative world – whether we have ever been there or not,"[4] due primarily to the widespread and ancient power of the Bible narrative, and, more recently, to increasingly frequent television and other communication exposure. Because of tradition, politics and the media, an inverse ratio exists between Israel's actual size and the place it occupies in the eyes of Israelis and foreigners alike.

In Israel "too much time has been spent over too little space,"[5] whereas in Canada a different disproportion applies: "vast distances, colossal size and above all, the absence of human beings and human scale," and a sense that though "seductive in its beauty, fearsome in its splendour,"[6] Canadian nature has not yet become saturated by human activity (ignoring, for the time being, ecological damage). Whereas every stone in the holy land of Israel has been overturned, built with, trodden upon and occasionally thrown by, or at, generations of religious Jews, Palestinian youths and/or Christian collectors of relics, about 90 percent of Canadian land is unowned.[7] Between this "unutterable silence,"[8] and the incessant tumult of battle cries and loud prayers emanating from Israel, and despite the innumerable ethnic, geographic, cultural and mental differences, there are still a few striking similarities between Canadians and Israelis where drama and theatre are concerned.

A key notion used by many Canadians and Israelis is the word *survival*. Northrop Frye, Margaret Atwood and Pierre Berton, three celebrated Canadian voices, and Israeli statesmen and writers such as Ben-Gurion, Amos Oz, and Amos Elon, emphasize the motif of survival as a dominant one in the Canadian and the Israeli consciousness respectively. While individuals may have reservations about such national characterization, on a collective, less immediate level, one can easily observe the attraction both nations have felt towards this particularly charged mode of perceiving their respective existences.

In Israel, as a consequence of the hardships and wanderings of the Jewish people, the term "survival" is mainly historical in significance. In "yearning to follow a moving frontier,"[9] on the other hand, Canadians express at least some of their sense of survival in images of a retreating space, that continually moves *away* from them, and the physical size of which is only one aspect of an immanent sense of *loss*. In Israel the opposite can be observed: space restrictions and closed-in frontiers threaten to renew the sense of siege in its inhabitants, who, historically, have only recently left their various Jewish enclaves behind them.

However, drama, as a genre meant for theatrical performance, demands an actual space on a stage. Such a space is physically real; yet it also represents a fictional and imaginary space which expresses and absorbs all that is directed from stage to audience and back to stage. As a "multi-"artistic medium – sets, movement, music, lighting, speech, dance, etc. – theatre is also a public place, medium and event. As such it is founded on a dialogue that is not only verbal, but also comprises the various theatrical languages, or modes of intercommunication, including the subtle, hinted, desired dialogue between stage and audience, and, finally, an implicit dialogue between the entire "house" and the street, the city, the social, political, ideological and religious aurae surrounding any theatrical event.

In Aristotelian terms, the ancient Greeks maintained a "classical" balance between the (somewhat inexact) unities of time, place and plot. In extending the image, one may conclude that Canadians have received a lot of place but little time for their plot; and Jewish Israelis a great deal of time for theirs, but only a tiny space. Canada and Israel are both immigrant countries, in which people are obliged, often as communities, and certainly as nations, to shape their given spaces for themselves. As such, both countries have a tremendously rich multi-cultural potential, heterogeneous and also very problematic. Both are relatively new nations whose citizens are attempting to form their new national identity while still retaining some, at least, of the imported and no less authentic modes of the world they have left behind.

In both countries theatre is a relatively new phenomenon, yet the actual beginnings are surprisingly close to one another. The first play ever written in Hebrew (1595)[10] was probably known about ten years before the first Canadian play was staged in Port Royal (1606).[11] Truly Canadian and Hebrew–Israeli theatre, however, had to wait about 300 years before it really flourished.[12] Because of its multi-medium character and inevitable dialogue, theatre requires historical as well as psychological perspective, or at least a minimal "distance," in order to express its time and space. In Canadian and Israeli theatre such perspective is especially needed to achieve an accurate expression of the typically dramatic conflicts that rise in an immigrant society. At the same time, whatever its "space," theatre should be regarded as a part of and an expression of national identity.

Both Canadian and Israeli modern drama is strongly influenced by traditional theatre techniques, styles and sub-genres. The first Hebrew-speaking group (later to become the Israeli national theatre *Habima*) was founded in Moscow after the first World War (with a performance of *The Dybbuk*) under the influence of Russian traditions mixed with German expressionism. The Irish Abbey Theatre served as a positive model for Canada;[13] and in later years both theatres acquired a great deal from English, French, Scandinavian, American and other traditions. Still lacking their own authentic modes, Canada and Israel each became meeting points between inevitable foreign influences, various models for imitation, and the growing wish for an independent expression of original form and content. Since in theatre, as in any other art, "form" and "content" are primarily metaphors for one another, foreign modes are borrowed and plundered to express particular, local and regional issues. However, the attempts to walk on stage in borrowed shoes often proved irritating, since the shoe did not always fit. Consequently there have been incessant discussions as to whether theatre in Canada and Israel should perform well tested, seasoned, imported plays, already proven successful artistically and (very important!) commercially; or whether they should attempt the more arduous effort of indigenous expression, immature as it may be.

European Jews have been involved in theatre for some 200 years, as directors, actors, musicians, etc. since their liberation from the ghetto in the late eighteenth century. Theatre in Hebrew, of course, is much younger, but translations, adaptations and original plays were mounted by amateur and professional groups since the beginning of the century, in what was then Palestine, under the Ottomans and the British mandate, as a metonymy for national revival, and an integral part of it. As late as 1945 there were still no professional Canadian theatre companies. The starting point of modern French Canadian drama is 1948, and of English Canadian drama 1967. The year 1948, marking the independence of the state of Israel, also marked the beginning of Israeli drama, increasingly written and acted by people born in the country, second generation to the original immigrants. The late beginnings in both countries added a sense of urgency, intensity and zest, not always compatible with professional criteria. Nevertheless, the immediate relevance of some of the new plays, in the first years, was rightly considered adequate compensation for quality, "because it is ours." Besides, a theatre expressing an *inward* examination, looking for values of a new ethnic, national and social identity, is sometimes a commercial non-entity in the international stock market of productions; and often in the local market too. Whereas traditional dramatic rites and rituals may find potential spectators even thousands of miles from their source, Israeli and Canadian theatrical qualms of identity tend to interest only those directly involved. Perhaps they are not exotic enough to attract outsiders.

While Canada and Israel both spent many formative years under British rule, Canadians were more influenced by English theatre, due both to the origin of many Canadians and to the much greater and longer-lasting impact of British colonial culture. Traces of theatrical colonialism can still be found in certain Canadian and also in Israeli productions, as in the Ontario Stratford Festival and the Cameri theatre in Tel Aviv. To this very day many Canadians and Israelis cross the Atlantic and the Mediterranean to see "really good theatre," the well-made plays and musicals of London's West

End. It is interesting to note that the English director Tyron Guthrie spent some time in Canadian and Israeli theatres in the 1950s, initiating the locals into the secrets of the art. Although plays by Robertson Davies and George Walker can be called "English," the latter has a more uniquely Canadian (as well as universal and personal) approach to drama, using a different kind of theatrical syntax. By the same token, Shulamit Lapid writes a "biblical" play based on the story of Abraham and Sarah in Genesis, but located in Palestine of the thirties and with dramatic personae of British Mandate officers.

With or without British colonial traditions, the immigrants' encounters with the inhabitants of Canada and Palestine reinforced their need for self-definition as Canadians or Israelis. Whether liberals or exclusivists, playwrights manipulated Indians and Inuit, Bedouin and Palestinian peasants, with a mixture of naïveté, ignorance and deliberate distortion, into figures serving as projections for newcomer attitudes.

Israeli playwrights of the "first settlement" years (around 1910) imposed upon the Arabs, those inhabitants they were somewhat surprised to find in the "Land of Their Fathers," many of the biblical myths they themselves wanted to acquire together with the land they settled on. Canadian playwrights must have been equally fascinated by Indian costumes, noble savages, swiftly galloping horses and many more such previously unencountered civilizational patterns, filtered through romantic notions and a much less romantic reality. Real wars were fought over lands and forests. In the real yet fictional and imaginary space on stage these aspects were presented with varying degrees of criticism and identification (with either side of the conflict), by playwrights, actors and audiences. Often those playwrights who were most identified with Canadianism, pioneering and Zionism, were also the most critical of the ways in which indigenous and minority peoples were treated.

It is not surprising that prevalent motifs in Canadian and Israeli drama are concerned with immigration, estrangement, minorities and families; with the family perceived as the only stable social unit in a new environment in Canada, and, because of ideological reasons, in the small community in Israel. It is felt, simultaneously, that in both cases the family unit is not only influenced by the surroundings, but also leaves its mark on it, thus creating a mediating rapport between people and their new land. In Canada and Israel one can also observe a relatively strong inclination towards documentary drama, the underlying assumptions of which are not simplified "realism," but rather a less secure attitude towards the gap between reality and theatrical fantasy. Historical drama too has been a characteristic feature, perhaps since both nations want to plan their future through presenting their past to the present; extending their real or invented "national time" with the help of fictional stage-time.

Radiophonic drama has its own special place. It played an enormous role in unifying Canada and in Israel it pioneered further theatrical performances. Notwithstanding the specific medium-oriented art of the radio play, it functioned as a type of theatre, bringing people the best available scripts and casts, under the respective politics and ideological guidance of the Canadian Broadcasting Corporation and Kol Israel ("The Voice of Israel").[14] Particularly interesting, but beyond the scope of this study, is the kind of space created by the radio play, which in Canada, very generally speaking, drew the vast expanses together while in Israel it tried to reach far beyond the actual borders.

Since television and video have taken over radio's role of catering to mass audiences, theatre has become free to study itself and its uniqueness, dealing more and more with its own artifice, public, and modes of message delivery. In both Canada and Israel a kind of theatre has emerged that examines itself while scrutinizing its society and environment. Increasingly self referential, Canadian and Israeli theatre also reveal a tendency towards deconstruction, especially in recent years. In breaking up the traditional well-made play into seemingly unrelated scenes (following, for example, Brechtian structural techniques), theatre invites the audience to participate more actively in supplying meanings, thus becoming more involved and more committed. This collage-styled theatre may also present a more democratic facade, less directly didactic, and relying on people's intelligence and sensitivity in subtler ways. In going to a theatre with a higher degree of self-reflection, spectators too are required to delve one step deeper into themselves.

Unlike written literature, which is "enacted" solely in the reader's imagination, a production is an actualized sociological event held in a public place and using dialogue as its major communicative tool. Non-verbal elements such as the use of space (including props, sets and costumes), movement, lighting and sound effects are as important to our analysis as the written text. All these elements are intrinsic aspects of a production and, in effect, theatrical metaphors of a play's meaning and message.

In a production there is no direct contact between audience and text. The text is mediated through the director, set designer, music composer, and the actors. Textual ambiguities are resolved by the production's executors and planners; non-verbal ambiguities are resolved not, as in the case of a poem, by readers in their own time and in the privacy of their homes, but in the immediacy of a public theatre, by the audience, whose very real presence is one of the major factors that allow a production to work. A production is thus an actual, concrete event with its own forms of expression, related more to the specific production than to the yet unrealized ideas that exist in the text as mere potentialities.

As a multi-system, theatre is a particularly difficult medium to compare cross-culturally. In addition to the various elements of theatre and their on-stage "dialogues," the meaning of their specific signs to specific audiences, one must also consider the interplay of text, subtext and context in any given production. This book attempts to treat some of these complexities, mainly through a comparative examination of theatre space.

The first chapter focuses on theatre space as a relation between offstage and on-stage space, laying the methodological ground for four more specific features of space treated in succeeding chapters: local and universal spaces, mythical space as seen through pathos and irony, the space of the indigenous stranger, and manifestations of social space.

I do not attempt to evaluate Canadian and Israeli plays according to purely artistic or qualitative criteria, because one of my main assumptions is that the intrinsic value of a play in both countries is socio-artistic, a reflection as well as a formative force in the consciousness of a relatively new "national theatre." Therefore the observations made are delineations of characteristics rather than rigid definitions.

The material for observation is, first, a body of some fifty Canadian plays, most of which appear in published and widely-known Canadian anthologies compiled by Canadian theatre people and scholars. One may well assume that, like any anthology, these reflect personal taste, and a fair amount of culture-politics; but they also contain an excellent variety of motifs and expressive modes, genres, conflicts and periods, Canadian regions and sensitivities. Quite obviously, the Canadians determine what they feel is "representative" in their drama, and the Canadian cross section of plays can thus be seen as what Canadians "dramatize" for themselves. The Hebrew–Israeli plays to be compared on the other side of the equation, were chosen by myself, from among several hundred. I have tried to use plays that achieved at least a minimal degree of public and professional attention, and match them with plays on the Canadian side, according to their specific treatment of space. The method adopted is, consequently, partly semiotic in nature[15] and partly based on a close reading of a dramatic text meant for performance. It is in this respect that I attempt to deal with Canadian open dramatic spaces and Israeli closed ones through criteria of the local and the universal.

Inside and outside the Canadian garrison and the Israeli bunker live people in need of inter-spacial dialogues. Garrisons and bunkers signify, in their respective geographical and social contexts, the unattainability of the space around them, space that is "escaping" or "besieging." Open and closed spaces can hence be seen as the main theme. Frye mentions the fear of nature;[16] Amos Elon devoted a special chapter of his book to the Israeli craze for archeological excavation,[17] seen as a semi-conscious wish to reassert their roots in and under the ground of their land. As an image, the Canadian North acts as "offstage" to the strip along the US border where most Canadians live. Having no such North, Israelis look for their offstage below the earth, but both nations seek a celestial offstage somewhere in the air. In drama, attempts are made to revive the land not only in writing[18] but in staging actual performances. This book is meant to be a small step on the path from stage to audience, and another step from the *on stage* theatre space to the *offstage* outside, here, there and everywhere.

1

Offstage: Space as a Present Void

One of the characteristic lines of development in modern theatre is theatre's interest in itself, its modes of expression and its addressees, the audience. This concern focuses on the relationship between theatre as imitating reality on the one hand, and creating new realities on the other, and on an increasing examination of the self-conscious fictionality of theatre and the real ability of that fictionality to refer to a world outside the stage, the auditorium, the church or the amphitheatre. Already in the Greek classical theatre, Aristophanes in *Peace* made his spectators conscious of the fact that he was well aware of presenting a theatrical show; almost all the scripts of the commedia del l'arte flaunt the artifice of theatricality in front of the audience. In Molière's *Grand Divertissement royal de Versailles*, there is a show within a show, a space within a space, both simultaneously fictional and real, combining various degrees of reality and the corresponding modes in which to perceive that reality, inserted one inside the other, and all within the framework of the activated space of theatre.

From medieval times on, theatrical modes of expression have developed as techniques, sometimes as images or metaphors serving various meanings, but also creating themselves in new forms of expression through sets, costumes, lighting and the elaborate mechanics of the stage. Our own century has seen different ways of acknowledging the presence of the audience: "poor theatre" (Grotowski), "cruel theatre" (Artaud), "epic theatre" (Brecht), "absurd" theatre (according to Esslin), as well as the theatre of events, street, protest, silence, joy, war, revolution, theatre for one person, for the masses, various forms of committed theatre as well as theatre of the bizarre, the initiatory and the sacred. Each and every one of these theatres expects, while evoking the audience's involvement and response, a different sort of participation between stage and auditorium.

While a written text uses literary discrepancies[1] in an active way, gaps through which the reader is prompted to participation, theatre, as a performing medium, relies on the dialogue occurring in an immediate, present, here and now; as an event in which "gaps of significance" are to be filled by understanding, feeling and perhaps even will; for the duration of the event presented and for some time after it ends. From the very delineation of space, which is binding for any theatre, it ensues that plays fill empty spaces and organize them, manipulate them, and design them.[2] Performed plays do this by using actual human presence, expressed mainly in word and movement. Space, therefore, can be perceived as the main metaphor for theatrical occurrence, as the "main mask" of dramatic activity: it is "itself and not itself" at the same time. From the establishment of theatrical location developed not only the modification of the onstage area, namely, the place on which theatrical activity was chosen to be shown, to present or to create a world, but and no less important, also what was chosen to remain offstage. "Sculpting in void," to paraphrase Peter Brook,[3] forms not only the onstage existence but also cleaves something from the outer "nothingness" and forms it, derives from it, relates to it, and contributes to it in an active way. The often ironic attempts of modern self-referential theatre to ignore its audience, as in the plays of Pirandello, Handke, Weiss, Stoppard and Beckett – as though maintaining that "stage represents only a stage" is a highly internalized argument equivalent to "all the world's a stage" – are based on a deliberate, sometimes humorous denial of the outside world rather than a real absence of it. Thus the tension between the outside of the world and the inside of the theatre is doubly emphasized. The solipsistic presumption which ensues from such existential attitudes towards theatre is mainly addressed against the quasi-exclusive mimetic aspect of theatre and not against its poetic one. According to this argument, no doubt a performative one, theatre becomes a competitor to the outside world. The importance of the stage is not its ability to reconstruct the world outside, but its ability to be a substitute for it, and to go beyond it.[4]

If the stage is the playing area, sets and props, then around it there exists an unseen realm,[5] an area from which the stage is activated, from and into which actors emerge during the show, from and into which sets and props are moved. It contains the flies, and the background effects to whatever is happening on the stage; and its precise technical borders, its character, functions and ways of action are determined in a relationship of neutral conditioning with the *what* and the *how* onstage. This area is the black aura of stage, *offstage*. It is the void, the specific "nothingness" surrounding the stage, nourishing the foetus as its placenta. Sometimes it serves as a cushion between reality and the theatrical event. In a book offstage is the literary gap; in music it can be the silence between the tones; in painting it is perhaps the canvas spread on the frame; in dancing it may be described as the "freeze," the lack of movement.

Offstage is not only an unseen, technical stage-space or the imaginary fictional space of the spectator but the actual realization of stage void. Insofar as a gap is the nothingness present in literature, so offstage is the "presentification" of theatrical absence. It is pure space which by its very essence actualizes the "non-there" and is formed according to the wishes, imaginations and projections not only of theatre people, but also of each and every individual member of the audience. Offstage is that theatrical element that demands individual loading, and can be seen also as a counter-balance against the herd instincts of the audience as a group. It is to offstage that every spectator projects imaginary props drawn from the storage in the back of the mind, completing that which happens onstage with the active help of that which is *not* happening there, but in his or her own head. Offstage is a *particular* silence about which one cannot speak, to quote Wittgenstein,[6] in a way which varies even from one performance to another. There is a necessary relationship between offstage and a number of aesthetic, existential and epistemological aspects and programmes of artistic representation in theatrical performances.[7]

As a primary "typology of offstage," one can list a number of types of this presented theatrical gap. A playwright may choose not to show certain things on stage, whether as a deliberate hiatus in the plot, or as a *telling* rather than showing technique, related to "outside" occurrences. A director, using any particular convention compatible with a period or personal style, may choose not to show other things onstage, even though they are written in the text. Either way, through deliberate choice, the stage can encompass only a small section of any real or imaginary existence, from the points of view of time, space, plot, the biography of the characters and obviously, from a purely technical point of view. One can also mention various sorts of personal offstage, such as offstage in a "show within a show," or of internal physical spaces unattainable to the audience either visually or acoustically. There is also an offstage of technical activation of the stage itself, harnessed for the manipulation of meaning. A special link exists between the high degree of self-referentiality of modern theatre and the intensive use made of offstage, operating those famous onion peelings of Ibsen's *Peer Gynt*; both the *I* and the theatre undergo a process of "peeling" in order to achieve a human, spiritual, non-material essence. This essence is both personal and individual, for the playwright, director, actors and members of the audience; it is a striving for the true self. For the same reasons it is totally universal.

In a more organic, holistic, dynamic and unified world view than we hold today, offstage was seen in dramatic tradition as part of a total integral system. Theatre scholars see a direct connection between religious rituals and rites, festivities of fertility and nature and processes of individual and group initiation, and the beginnings of theatre – as in the funeral ceremonies of ancient Egypt, Babylon and Syria, in Orphic and Eleusian mysteries, or in dithyrambic processions, etc.[8] In all these the spatial elements as well as time, costume, holy objects, actions and gestures that happen *in* the space, are perceived as a bridge between the here and now, and the there and beyond. The perception of space reflects a world view that has experienced the consciousness of the supernatural no less than that of the physical and sensual world. Whereas an initiation rite, for instance, uses manipulations of physical reality in order to reach meta-physical essences, the growing adherence to materialism throughout the generations, with the subsequent technological development that is both a result and a cause of it, enhance the differences between the spiritual and physical realms from the point of view of space as well. When humanity started to doubt the absoluteness, objectivity and commitment imposed by a system of belief in spiritual forces, human consciousness itself became increasingly active and consequently more focused on its own strength. Concomitantly, the gap between space experienced as a kind of a spiritual womb in which in and out are less distinguished from each other, and actual space was presented as material, internal and conscious, leaving an outside space which became strange, unclear and sometimes either divine and as such blurred, distanced, dubious, or even totally bereft of existence. With the development of theatre, the perception of theatrical space naturally also developed. Parallel to a gradually growing self-referential mode that has dominated human consciousness and its artistic expressions in general and theatre in particular, a perception of space developed as that which is directly experienced, actually present, characterizing the immediacy and "presentness" of the medium of theatre.

Whoever studies Genet, Chekhov, Beckett and even Goethe and Shakespeare, Calderon de la Barca, and Molière, is soon convinced of the high degree of self-reference in their works.[9] Accordingly, one encounters a compatible perception of space which forms and especially locates, such self-reflection. First, however, in order to focus on modern elements in "universal" theatre, and then in more local works by Canadian and Israeli playwrights, we should briefly scan the history of offstage. To the question how, whether and what should be performed onstage, and what is important, worthwhile or interesting to locate (or leave) offstage, different periods and places have given different answers, especially in practical terms.

When the palace door opens, the bleeding corpses of Agamemnon and Cassandra in Aeschylus are brought to front stage after they have been slain outside. Oedipus' eyes are plucked out offstage, and it is "there" that he exchanges sight for insight. Classical Greek plays often open with an exposition of offstage, introducing other times and spaces into stage present; often too offstage is used in the beginning of a play as a technique for establishing location. Strength's first line to Hephaistos in Aeschylus' *Prometheus Bound* is "Here we have reached the remotest region of the earth." The nurse in Euripides' *Medea* says: "If only they had never gone! If the Argo's hull never had winged out . . . towards Colchis!" The choir in *Persians* draws a long horizontal line from Greece to the Persian king's palace; and Dionysus himself, the protagonist of the *Bacchae*, draws a vertical line in describing lightning from heaven striking the land in "this city of Thebes." Expressing doubt that Dionysus is the true son of Zeus is the *hubris* and the main theme of the play. At the same time, in theatrical terms, this also implies doubting offstage. Therefore Dionysus "will plague them with madness." The *Bacchae* is a ritual play which confronts the divine, offstage point of view with the human, "onstage" one. As a sophisticated playwright accepting belief in the divine, at least for the sake of this play, Euripides presents *hubris* and stupidity, as well as the pain caused by this scepticism. Offstage here is in fact an actual expression of divinity, which also contains the relationship between the dramatic element and the "staging" of the God.

Since classical Greek drama was religious, not excluding its apparently atheistic aspects, such as rebellion against divinity, it is not surprising that offstage was not only a function of technical limitations or even of classical aesthetics. Medea's children, for instance, are not murdered onstage for quite complex reasons. Certainly the Greek audience was much more moved by such a crime when it did *not* see it. It was well understood that the performance of a fictional murder, however convincingly carried out, is not "real." In such cases, the imagination is far more fertile, efficient, wild and fear-inspiring. Moral and sexual atrocities, defecation and obscenities, namely matters within the categories of moral and behavioral taboos, were therefore doomed to remain offstage in theatre then and (almost) ever since. It is plausible, therefore, that the exile to which Medea, Oedipus and many other protagonists were sentenced, was and is a most fitting dramatic punishment (it was probably also acceptable from an historical point of view); exile being a space, the most important feature of which is *not being here*. But while Medea will go as far as the country of Erechtheus, and Jason her husband will be killed by a plank falling on his head on the Argos – both of them offstage – the physical blindness of Oedipus compels him to carry the recognition of the results of his sin as if it were clear-sightedness, as an onstage internalization of offstage occurrences. He does not go offstage; rather offstage enters him. Already in this play in the early history of the theatre, offstage can be distinguished as existing not only outside the stage, but also deep inside it, provided that certain matters remain unexpressed, unactualized, and only hinted at, and therefore rich in imaginary possibilities and inviting gap-filling processes in the spectator.

The Romans, considered by some theatre historians as more rational, perceived space as a more material entity, more contracted into its here and now. The children of the Roman *Medea* are slaughtered *onstage*. Seneca's play ends with a description of a heroine who is used to exile, but Jason's last words are ambiguous from the point of view of the very existence of offstage, in a non-psychological way. "Go on through the lofty spaces of high heaven and hear witness, where thou ridest, that there are no Gods."[10] Commenting on the neo-classical version of "not being here" in Racine's *Phedre*, which is no different from that of Medea, Ann Ubersfeld emphasizes the emptiness of space and that which ought to be presented scenically on stage as a concrete "no space," "no picture." Although she herself does not reify offstage, only a small jump towards the conclusion presented here is missing: stage void exists and is present in its absence, in the use of offstage.[11]

In the Middle Ages certain sorts of stages exemplified the various planes of reality. The terrestrial present was placed in the centre, heaven and paradise usually on the right, hell on the left. Mundane scenes were always located between the extremes[12] as if to say that humanity is doomed here in this world to a short, intensive and highly binding choice between the two sorts of eternity offered to it in the world beyond. Sometimes when shows were mounted on pageant carts, location was presented vertically, and so the value-charged image of up–down reinforced the religious existential message. Stage, as a special formation, translated the a-temporal perception of reality as a co-existence of past, present and future into static, simultaneous location. Paradise and Hell, the Temple and the Golden Gate, Herod's palace as a chair and the entire Jerusalem as a small house, were all visually presented. The stage did not presume to represent naturalism in an earthly sense. On the contrary, it was through this ideologically efficient use of its very limitations that the stage signified the reality of the beyond, in exposing the wretched and worldly nature of earthly objects. There, here and now are nothing but a passing moment and death plucks souls like flowers, as recounted in *Everyman*.

When medieval performances started to emerge from the space of the church out onto the town square, the church itself, still physically and mentally in the background, served as offstage to the show, being the actual source of power of that which was happening on stage. It was the divine message and the promised redemption standing behind the sometimes amusing and lighthearted theatrical event. As long as religious ceremonies like the original "Quem Queritas" were held within the church, the crypt, the arches, the stained glass windows, were all used as an organic part of the setting, highly metaphorical in their religious significance. Later, as the shows moved to the public square and became more secular, more entertaining in function, the church still knew how to harness even potential lasciviousness to the religious messages. While the reins were physically held by the Guilds, who planned the pageants and erected the sets and the machinery, the clergy guided the growing popularity of these events towards that which they themselves wanted to say, namely, to the reality of the real religious offstage, whether they actually believed in it or merely exploited it for their own reasons. Since a location such as the town square outside the church door naturally becomes desacralized, stories that include secular and often profane elements can be presented. As long as the church could manipulate the stage, it could also allow a certain degree of impudence, even towards itself, as in *The Second Shepherds' Play*. Even mockery was harnessed to the religious chariot in a still organic and holistic world view.[13]

Medieval entertainment was achieved through the public and mutual festive participation of actors and spectators who knew each other very well. It would appear to have been a festivity of all for all, not the climax of the story itself being the important issue but, rather, the entire annual process of representation, with its threats of offstage hell, and its chances of redemption. Contraptions such as the trap doors were metaphors for the snares of fate and the sins of carnal existence, while the machinery of the "secrets" provided an image for the eternal other option, redemption. Other technical elements, pyrotechnics and other effects were often very elaborate indeed. A Bourges performance (in 1536), needed three hundred people to manipulate the stage of "the deeds of the emissaries," which included human actors, ropes and boards, shapes and colors, such as the cross itself, which presented offstage messages and entities in a dynamic continuity. In the Christian world view in which flesh becomes spirit and vice-versa, it was relatively easy to receive official blessing for theatrical events constructed basically along the same principle: every plane of being is both a part of a reflection and a metaphor of any other plane.[14] Since many medieval theatre festivals were held on Corpus Christi, acts of theatrical trans-substantiation were fully compatible with the purely religious ones.

The hard work invested in the relatively brief presentation of the show, all the material elements, the financial and technical outlay and even the comic roles, were granted religious authorization thanks to the religious message. The stage became, firstly, a theatrical space in the architectural sense (pageant, carts, square, stage, etc.); secondly, a space treated in costumes, props and locations; and, thirdly, a dramatic space, as used by the group of actors.[15] Above these three types of space pure space could be sensed, sanctified, conditioning the event through its religious aura while absorbing the event into itself and maintaining a dialectic between profanity and sanctity.

Apart from Aristophanes, who did so in a satirical way, the Greeks did not often present the space of the Gods on their stages.

Rather they brought the Gods into their own terrestrial space of onstage. In the Middle Ages an inclination can be discerned to expand the stage into a temporary image of eternity in an attempt to bring it closer to the supertime and superspace of eternity itself. Onstage hints were planted, like the tangible edge of a spiritual iceberg, indicating what was to be expected in the beyond. Hundreds of years later Samuel Beckett would ponder in his pantomimes, *Act Without Words I and II*, on the who or what of the "flies," and would turn the activating techniques of offstage into the main subject matter of these two plays for movement. Medieval stage space represents an orderly, absolute and objective spiritual world, menacing if not accepted, but consoling and redeeming if mankind would only be willing to find refuge in its shelter. The main referentiality of such a theatre is that stretched between stage and offstage: it is entertaining, lighthearted, and easily digestible from the point of view of the outside towards the inside of the event on the stage; and it is also educational and binding on the way from the stage back out to the beyond, to the church, to Christ and to God, as far as what is *really* demanded of the audience. The physical, vulgar and actualized realm can thus be considered a mere corridor to an everlasting divine world. The stage achieves its power from the outside, and transmits its messages back to it.

Less than a hundred years after the Copernican revolution, as much a revolution of consciousness as it was an innovation in the scientific world view, the attitude between stage and offstage was equally revolutionized. Copernicus did not change the cosmic elements themselves but observed them, and expressed the relationships between them, in a different way. As it became accepted that the sun rather than the earth was at the centre of the cosmic system, a major shift occured not only in the position of the object observed, but also in the very observing consciousness of the viewer: the consciousness itself became the observed object. And so, despite a saddened awareness that we are no longer in the centre, we have been compensated by being able to focus on our own consciousness. Concomitantly, and for the next hundred years, changes in consciousness occured in other areas as well. Rembrandt started to paint self-portraits, and Cervantes to write about himself. Descartes turned self-consciousness and the act of doubting from a philosophical, psychological and artistic device into his very subject matter, and at the same time a lever with which to extract himself from endless perplexity.

In classical Greek theatre it was quite reasonable to bewail the hardships of human fate, and the arbitrariness of the gods dwelling in their Olympic offstage. While the gods were often described as nasty, murderous, and unfair, their actual being was never doubted. As offstage partners, to whom the performance was often dedicated, they may have been amused or even furious, but as far as the stage was concerned, there were at least some gods to talk to, if not with. As confidence in an absolute divine world crumbled, people in the theatre too, turned to their own self-consciousness, to the very process of creation, establishing it not as a Mimesis of an external given, but rather as a Poiesis, a competitive creation challenging the gods. Descartes first had to secure the eye looking at the world; Shakespeare let his readers and audiences be aware of his process of creation in the monologue "All the world's a stage"; in the "mousetrap" scene in *Hamlet*; and throughout *A Midsummer Night's Dream*, where a parallel exists between the *conscience positionelle* and the *conscience réfléchie* on the one hand, and stage and offstage on the other.

In a brilliant foreshadowing of what in the twentieth century would be a dominant mode, Shakespeare presents three levels of existence in *A Midsummer Night's Dream*, each of which – the court, the fairy world, and the actors' world – is shaped through a stage within a stage, acting, at the same time, as an offstage to each other. While Greek and medieval offstage express religious systems that demand a dialogue, in a more modern world, such as that shown by Shakespeare, these systems seem to have contracted into themselves, and the stage begins to deal with the void within itself. Shakespeare did not relinquish the Christian lever as an option for redemption, but the absoluteness of this "Archimedian" lever as an offstage symbol was shattered.

The "mousetrap" scene in *Hamlet* contains this multi-level: the pantomime preceding the play within the play functions towards the "mousetrap" as the "mousetrap" itself functions towards *Hamlet*, the play. On closer observation, role play can be discerned even within the preceding pantomime, thus revealing four planes of reality within reality that turn the eyes of the beholder inward into an inner psychological offstage, as well as towards some external justification. Both are intended to redeem the self, which is afraid of plunging self-reflectively into its own void. The projecting Elizabethan stage, empty as it was, can also be seen as an image of a shrinking offstage, the stage itself thrusting forward as though to receive help from the audience. The monologue of "All the world's a stage" in *As You Like It* and Hamlet's instructions to the actors about to play the "mousetrap," are delivered in a rational and conscious way, with the sense of connection between theatre and life holding less religious and much more psychological significance than in medieval theatre. It is in a way a Copernican theatrical revolution.

By the early nineteenth century, in Goethe's *Faust*, meticulous attention was being given to different sorts of offstage. The dedication after the opening of the first curtain is an expression of inner space (it is so, at least, in the Dornach production in Switzerland, which retains every detail of the original text), emphasizing the poet/playwright's private space: "All that I have, now far away seems banished,/All real grown, that long ago had vanished." It is a striking expression of the unattainability of the speaker's inner space. Then a second curtain opens, exposing the fictionality and the medium-oriented reality of the opening "theatre scene" in the play: "Within one boarded house's narrow bound, I mete out Creation's spacious round . . . "[16] A third curtain then opens to reveal yet another space in the play, in which the spectators are invited to mount heavenwards to a divine scene with God, the angels and Satan. Only after these three curtains have opened, revealing three "layers" of offstage, are we brought into the narrow, gothic chamber of Faust, pondering over his dull achievements in learning, while many spaces already enfold both the audience and the stage.

In the late nineteenth century, where exactly does Nora vanish to once she has slammed the door behind her in Ibsen's *A Doll's House*? Has she gone into some other human house, apparently offstage, or has she departed for the open world? To freedom? To solitude? In *Peer Gynt*, the more poetic play, the button-moulder's spoon is perhaps Peer's offstage; or is offstage here, in Ibsen's quest play the brinkmanship of Peer's fantastic leap onto the elk's back. In Wedekind's *Spring Awakening*, Melchior jumps from the realm dominated by spring, youth and life, into that of winter, aging and death. With this shift, Wedekind draws on to the stage a realm of existence which had remained offstage until its exposure at the end. In the twentieth century, in Pirandello's *Henry IV*, the protagonist chooses to lock himself into his inner offstage, avoiding encounter with the wickedness outside the imaginary castle in which his family has imprisoned him. Sanity and insanity provide each other here with mutual offstage entities. In *Six Characters in Search of an Author* Pirandello posits a series of competing realities challenging each other, on and offstage; Genet in *Veils* turns the inside out in a lucid and very effective stage artifice. He and Pirandello make the essence of fictionality the offstage to their stages. In *Before Breakfast*, Eugene O'Neill evokes the offstage existence of a character who, supposedly, dwells in a room adjacent to the stage, and is revealed only at the end, through the extending of a pale hand, shortly before committing suicide; outside, of course. Ionesco's *Rhinoceros* presents an offstage world which is nonetheless well heard, very close and extremely threatening, precisely because it is unseen. All the occurrences on stage would be quite futile and foolish without that outside. And indeed in his *Chairs*, the non-characters of the outside exist and dwell on stage. The words of the actual characters on stage prepare contours for the non-existent characters into which they are supposed to fit, and with which they play a game of theatrical presence and absence. Maeterlinck, in *The Blind*, creates a feeling that the mystical being in the forest hovers over his characters no less than over the audience, and the same is true for Ghelderode's *The Stranger*, in *Who's There* by Tardieu, and many plays by Pinter such as *The Dumb Waiter* and *The Caretaker*.

Tom Stoppard in *Rosenkrantz and Guildenstern are Dead* turns the stage totally inside out. His deliberate dependence on Shakespeare's *Hamlet* accentuates the use of the trick of internalizing offstage. Minor figures in Shakespeare, Rosenkrantz and Guildenstern are main characters with Stoppard. What in Shakespeare is a key, is here the lock: " . . . If you look on every exit being an entrance somewhere else."[17]

Peter Handke, one of the most extreme of playwrights in terms of manipulating offstage as well as self-reference, destroys even the realistic fallacy which stands at the threshold of every theatre at every performance. In his *Caspar*, "stage represents stage," quite explicitly. In *Offending the Audience*, the stage does not even "represent" a stage, rather it *is* simply a stage. In his *Ride Over Lake Constance*, a stage is presented as referring exclusively to itself, pretending total ignorance of any possible external world. The protagonists are the actual actors who just happen to appear in the production.

An active, particularly sophisticated, use of offstage can be seen in Samuel Beckett's plays, from *Waiting for Godot*, with the great guru of modern offstage, namely Godot himself, to the much more explicit threat cast by offstage in the last play, *What, Where*. *Endgame* relates to offstage as death, both through the window towards the "sea" and the window towards the "land." Winnie in *Happy Days* sinks into the offstage onstage, in her mound; up to her neck in the second act of that play, and to "her" mouth, in *Not I*, which can be considered as a third act to *Happy Days*. Krapp in *Krapp's Last Tape* plays at being on and offstage fairly actively. Beckett's plays clearly give the impression that the characters are not only sucked away towards offstage, by means of urns, ashbins, etc., but that, in a much more threatening way, offstage lurches nearer and nearer towards the audience and will soon devour them too.[18] It is very likely that the new identities with which Vladimir and Estragon play in *Waiting for Godot* are a Beckettian improvement on a Chekovian principle. It is the outside in Beckett's play that erases identity, and after a renewed entrance the character must update itself with details of time, space and personality. The plot itself is always outside in these plays.

The grounds for the extensive use of offstage in modern times were laid by Chekhov, one of whose most poignant formulations of offstage can be found in *The Seagull*. Chekhov, unlike Handke, Stoppard or Beckett, does not break away from the conventions, but the effectiveness of his theatrical devices is not impaired. Looking at some of the connections between stage and offstage in Chekhov's plays reveals his attitude to the problems and possibilities of presenting reality onstage, and also shows that quite a number of Canadian and Israeli playwrights and directors have made use of the modes he suggests, implicitly or explicitly, of treating offstage. In his complex and subtle way, Chekhov deals with self-reference when he activates offstage, positing the relation stage–offstage as reflecting the relationship theatre-life. A playwright in the predominantly realistic tradition on the one hand, and one who greatly influenced contemporary theatre on the other, Chekhov's treatment of offstage deserves a more extensive examination, as a test case.

Part of the negotiations between stage and offstage are held in the form of a dialogue between offstage voices and visual and auditive events onstage. Chekhov's plays contain dozens of such dialogues. Two sorts of voices can be discerned in *The Seagull*: those that both characters and audiences hear, and those that only the characters hear or imagine. For instance, when Treplev says he hears steps, Chekhov does not indicate that steps are actually heard. Arkadina claims that she hears singing from across the lake; nobody else, onstage or in the auditorium, hears anything at all. Medviedenko says "I seem to hear somebody crying there."

In other cases, Chekhov explicitly indicates characters' reactions to the voices meant only for the audience to hear. The sound of the string breaking in the second act of *The Cherry Orchard* is acknowledged: Lopakhin says, "I don't know, maybe somewhere in the mines . . . "; Gaiev reacts "Maybe some bird"; Andreyevna adds, "Quite unpleasant somehow"; and Firs adds, "a boiling kettle" as a possible interpretation of the strange noise. By this time this famous string breaks at the end of the play, a great deal of meaning has already been accumulated, and no additional interpretation is required. The significance of this gap must be completed by the audience. In the performance, Chekhov enables a subjective activation of offstage intended for the characters, at the same time enriching the personage with an original mode of depiction. On yet another level, he hints that each character has its own inner world, the voices of which only it is likely to hear. Therefore, offstage is a sign not only for what happens *outside*, but also for an inside to which others have no access.

Offstage voices can provide a suspense-creating element. When Treplev asks "Who's there?," the audience already knows what has happened and in this case offstage voices are multi-functional, acting as an indication of Treplev's sensitivity as well as a foreshadowing of future developments in the plot and preparation for the entrance of the next character, Nina. Against the background noises of trees and wind and melancholy piano playing, and other generally atmosphere-creating voices which also help the audience to relate more specifically to each character, three further sounds of knocking are discernible. Chekhov constructs them in an enhanced and ironic order. The play opens with sounds of coughing and knocking after which Masha and Medviedenko enter. The doorman knocks after it has been understood from Masha's words "Here Constantine Gavrilovich finds it more comfortable to work." The last "knocking" is the shot at the end of the play. This combination of knocks and shots is also found in *Uncle Vanya* and *The Three Sisters*, testifying to Chekhov's particular attention to the musical orchestration of offstage auditory effects.

In *The Three Sisters* further use is made of various sounds such as chimes, bells, the musical tones of a harmonica, piano, fiddle and harp, a lullaby to the baby, and voices in search. All these are heard more than once in the play, and are usually placed at strategically significant moments. Similarly, in *The Seagull* the killing shot is heard before it is explained by the dialogue.[19] On the other hand, unlike Treplev's shot, which is almost immediately accounted for, Tuzenbach's death is elucidated only by Chebutykin who enters later; in the meantime, also in order to enhance the impression, an orchestra is heard playing a march.

At the end of the third act a fairly long scene takes place, mostly in the realm of offstage. The sisters leave, one by one, behind onstage screens, effectively offstage spaces presented onstage, where they hold their conversations. The emptiness of the stage is particularly emphasized when the alarm bell is heard. Here the offstage noise, in the line given to Andrey, merges with the motif of disappointment for a happiness never to be achieved. Irina, on the other hand, announces that the brigade has been ordered away.

After a preparatory scene and a noise which perhaps was not heard – "Here I think they come," the audience actually hears the sound of the two approaching carriages and the bustle of entering. The movement of being swept from offstage to stage is balanced by a movement of being drawn offstage at the end of the play.

The final noise in Chekhov's last play, *The Cherry Orchard*, is described as a real sound, that of an axe banging on the tree, but a symbolic meaning is undoubtedly given to the twang of the breaking string as though it were "happening" in heaven. This sound ends a gradually growing series of offstage noises in the play. The same is true for *The Three Sisters* and *Uncle Vanya*. In Chekhov's more important plays, the ending is always a prolonged farewell scene. In *The Seagull* the end comes as a blow, in *Uncle Vanya* there is an ironic pseudo-satisfaction with the world of the stage, in remaining there and giving up the offstage in an attempt at survival. In *The Three Sisters* the conflict between stage and offstage – "The tune of the orchestra is slowly diminishing" – is presented as a yearning for other places. Moscow is that other place for the sisters, as Chebutykin's voice draws our attention to whatever remains onstage. Masha, Olga and Irina stand pressed against each other onstage, their yearning addressed to whatever is, and always will be, outside. In *The Cherry Orchard* it certainly seems that offstage has the upper hand since only Firs remains onstage, quite forgotten, as he himself says. Finally, he lies there motionless, enveloped in the emptiness of active nothingness, on a stage which has committed suicide, given itself up, turning as it were into a focus of offstage.

The frequent entrances and exits in Chekhov's plays have been thoroughly dealt with in the critical literature; their quality and quantity certainly draw special attention to offstage. Chekhov's characters, such as Nina, return to the stage after having undergone changes, sometimes crucial ones, offstage. Other characters were supposed or expected to undergo changes but never did, as in Gaiev's case or Andrey's, the brother of the three sisters, who prefers to remain offstage. Often he is called onto the stage, but "Some mannerism he's got, always to sneak away. Come here!" In the same play there are other characters whose mode of life is offstage or at its edges. Bobick, Andrey and Natasha's son, comes on stage only in a pram, never to be seen. He is no doubt one of the most interesting "not existing" characters, drawing attention to himself through his parents, his aunts, and the audience. Children, as common offstage figures, do not just "steal the show," but in fact can be more effective in their absence.

To eliminate an impression of chance concerning his intentions, Chekhov fills the play with further offstage figures: Vershinin's sick daughter and his suicidal wife; Protopopov who is mentioned seven times and never appears (is he the real offstage father of the offstage baby Bobick, rather than Andrey?); and also those who are called the masked figures, the wanderers. In *The Cherry Orchard* there is also a drunkard vagabond, probably an allegorical Russian figure, an important representative of offstage. These absent/present characters remind us of later characterizations in the symbolistic dramas of Maeterlinck, Magritte, Madame Rachilde, Yeats and many others. From a symbolistic point of view it is easier to deal with esoterics on stage, but Chekhov treads a more difficult path, cautiously navigating between symbolistic poetry and psychological realism.

Chekhov's plays are characterized by the tension between where they actually occur and those other places where the characters would prefer to live and spend their time; and especially *be*, physically, mentally and spiritually. The description of Old Basmanni Road where Vershinin lives is as realistic in Olga's eyes as her actual dwelling on stage. This offstage location does not remain on a metaphorical level only, as an image for a complete life full of meaning and satisfaction but always happening in other times and places. Chekhov deals with yearnings for the future, or longing for the past, both existing elsewhere from the necessary points of departure, as far as the here and now of the medium-oriented theatrical notion is concerned. He reifies the theatrical tautology of "only the present exists, the past was, and the future will be" and turns offstage into an active expression of whatever is not present and immediate; thus creating constant conflicts between stage presence and non-presentifiable offstage representatives.

In the play-within-a-play that Treplev shows on stage in *The Seagull*, there are a number of effects such as the lights of the swamp, the moonlight, the stars twinkling, piano music, which are later recalled in the scene between Treplev and Nina. What was a play within a play in the first act of *Seagull*, sometimes an offstage onstage, becomes in the fourth act theatrical material evoked as common memories for two characters. Between Nina and Treplev meetings take place on two levels and in two present tenses of the play: in the first act they meet on a fictional level as well as on the meta-fictional level, that of the play-within-the-play. Two years later they meet again but in the meantime Nina has managed to become pregnant, lose her child and fail as an actress in offstage times and spaces. Chekhov intertwines offstage occurrences with onstage activities. Nina and Treplev's meetings are full of discrepancies and failed intentions, which are partly to blame for Treplev's suicide. Towards the end of the third act, Chekhov once again turns onstage happenings into offstage. The chambermaid takes away a basket of plums, and Trigorin returns to fetch his walking stick, while from behind the stage the sounds of departure can be heard. Nina and Trigorin are therefore able to say farewell and arrange a future meeting, downstage. This flexible use of offstage makes it possible to characterize both the similarities and the differences between the characters both in Treplev's play-within-the-play and in *The Seagull* itself: Treplev–Nina, Trigorin–Arcadina, Nina–Trigorin, while using the difference between what happens to them onstage and offstage.

In *The Three Sisters*, an offstage fire is the realization of a metaphor of what happens onstage. The fire reaches the stage in the form of alarm bells, through which the audience learns of the characters' inner sparks. This is a fire which never breaks out. The fire in the city, like the garden in *The Cherry Orchard*, and the sets for Treplev's play-within-a-play in *The Seagull* are a broader offstage aura, based on ideological and philosophical ponderings in Vershinin's, Astrov's and Trophimov's respective manners; they are musings about a promising offstage future. Whether "great darkness" pervades there or not, the characters are doomed never to find out.

The gaps between stage and offstage enable Chekhov to present onstage events as *present activity*, which is immediate, hopeless and futureless, whereas the classical dramatic *action*, likely to change things, and bring about shifts in the plot, will always remain outside. The question of genre – realistic, fantastic, poetic, etc. – which has occupied the minds of many Chekhov scholars, can also be examined in terms of stage activity versus offstage inactivity. His onstage characters usually do not have the necessary will-power to bring about real action, and the consequent tragic flaw, crisis, and "blow to the consciousness" (Anagnorisis) thus occur as in classical drama. Some changes may occur offstage too, but it is the deliberate use of the banal onstage in the light of what does not happen on it, which gives Chekhov's plays the right to stand as a genre on their own. Chekhov's stage is always here and now, but it does indeed have the osmotic ability to absorb things from the outside. According to Chekhov's theatrical syntax, it is not surprising that Irina always says "And incessantly you have the feeling that you are getting farther and father away from the real, beautiful life, always far away, far far towards some abyss." In Nina's words to Treplev, we find an explicit exposure of the theatrical device which also reveals the relationship between what is onstage and off it.

"He didn't believe in the stage (. . .) I became trivial and common-place; I acted without meaning . . . I did not know what to do with my hands, or how to stand on the stage, I had no control over my voice. You can't imagine how you feel when you know that you are acting atrociously . . . What was I talking about? Ah about acting. I'm not like now . . . I'm a real actress now . . . The chief thing is not fame or glory, not what I dreamed of, but the gift of patience. One must bear one's cross and have faith."

In Nina's speech, Chekhov hypothesizes offstage onstage. Nina's self realization as an actress takes place, if it does, on a stage outside the stage of this play. When Andrey in *The Three Sisters* says "I'm sick of the present," he may appear as a strange precursor of Beckett's Krapp, who stands "late in the evening in the future," hopelessly trying to bridge his present onstage existence with an irretrievable past and a doubtful and short future. Both past and future have no real existence on any stage of any theatre whatsoever. Chekhov provides an abundance of offstage signs in his plays, to enhance the effect of the tantalizing torment of his characters. They are doomed to a life of everlasting stage existence, like Pirandello's people, who look for their author outside of the theatre.

Messages from the offstage world arrive as telegrams and letters hidden in little offstage spaces on stage; in closets the keys to which are lost. Thus these closets become little stages without keys. The systematic exposure of offstage phenomena is a typical Chekhovian device; almost every offstage sign, even the atmospheric sound of wind and storm, is given an actual realistic interpretation onstage. But this is indeed walking a tightrope between fiction and realism and unsentimental ironic symbolism. Charlotte Ivanovna's magic tricks in evoking strange voices, in hiding and revealing herself somewhere else and in extracting Anya from behind the screen (*The Cherry Orchard*), seem to be the nearest manifestation to what Chekhov himself does: connecting the here and now with a there and then; moulding the stage in constant, conscious and creative relation to what is not on it.

Perhaps one of Chekhov's most important contributions to modern playwriting, and especially to the genre called "absurd," is the presentation of absence, namely, the Parmenidian attempt to claim "nothingness exists" in theatrical terms. His influence cannot be properly evaluated simply because it is too great. As a generalization one may say that playwrights all over the world are deeply indebted to him, consciously or not, and among them one finds quite a number of Canadians and Israelis.

2

Local and Universal Space

The tension between the universal and the specifically local aspects of plays is expressed in the relationship between onstage and offstage occurrences. This is not the only expression of the discrepancy between the universal and the local, but from a theatrical point of view, which differs from the dramatic generic one, it is dominant. Offstage is indeed the main area demanding interpretation in the *performed* play. It is that which invites the specific, sometimes also local, personal or ideological, filling of gaps, where the spectator maintains an active dialogue not only with whatever is concretely presented onstage, and therefore complete, but also a dialogue with that which is not there. Between the individual and universal characteristics of offstage, on the one hand, and stage, necessarily committing itself to particular choices of sets and spaces, thus making them "local," on the other, there is a dialogue requiring a high degree of audience involvement.

Since the performances seen by most audiences in the world are imported, in terms of time, space and especially milieu, there is additional interest to a discussion of the cultural shifts that affect plays. Unlike written literature which is "performed" in the reader's own imagination, in a time and place of one's own choosing, a theatre show is a social and dialogical event. Therefore the cultural shift discussed here is not in drama as a literary genre, but in theatre as a medium, necessitating an examination not only of the text, but also of the non-verbal elements such as space (including sets, props, and costumes); movement and lighting, music and sound effects. All these are expressive means acting as metaphors for the messages of the play in its entirety.

The text of a play moving from one culture to another is no more problematic than that of a story or a poem, but a production follows different rules since the connection between text and audience is mediated by the director, set designer, musician, and especially the actors. Important gaps in the playwright's text are filled by the planners of the production and the participants, and new gaps, many of which are non-verbal, open up instead, intended to be filled not by a reader (implied from the playwright's point of view) but by an audience, whose very presence and active participation make the event itself possible. The live immediate dialogue happening here and now is the crucial factor in theatre. The show is an actualized event which must have form, expressive means and messages specific to the time and place of the event, while also fulfilling the potentiality of the original text.[1]

Theatrical gaps, as we have seen, are manifested through off-stage. Assuming that the show indeed precisely follows the stage directions of the author in any particular "local" play, an audience not directly familiar with the particular milieu of a Chekhovian petty aristocratic country house in Tsarist Russia, plays, can still understand and identify with whatever is there but not presented: the offstage of the inner souls of the characters; and that outside offstage aura which is ready to absorb "non-local" projections of the audience.

As an example, Beckett's Godot can be an image of the Palestinian revolution as in Ilan Ronen's 1954 production in Haifa, giving the play a specific political interpretation; or a wish for a Communist revolution; a hope for national revival during the *glasnost* period; liberation from jail as in the St. Quentin production; an image of woman's liberation as in the feminist Montreal production in 1976; a yearning for religion in a secular age, or any one of many other possibilities as the endless productions of this play testify. Many, even contrasting, interpretations may stick to plays such as this one, rich with offstage indeterminacies: the so-called "absurd" plays[2] are characterized by relatively few local specificities and they excel in deliberate indefiniteness of time and space. The genre of the absurd had an understandably short, but intensive life. It was intensive because it renovated modes of theatrical expression, and short because it was admitted retrospectively that regular audiences, other than marginals and avant-garde intellectuals, do not par-ticularly frequent universalistic absurd shows unconnected to a particular reality or emotionally identifiable, at least on a local basis. Except for a few rare cases, such as Ionesco and Beckett, nowadays "absurd" plays are not often performed by commercial and repertory theatres.

On a stage, figures need a specific flesh and blood, even if
fictional, characterization. The local aspect does not necessarily
impinge but may rather be the catalyst of a universal message, since
"people in general" do not exist but are always born, grow up and
develop under specific circumstances of inheritance, surroundings,
upbringing and individuation. Sometimes the mention of the scent
of a particular grass growing somewhere in the Canadian prairies,
unfamiliar to anyone but the indigenous people of the region, can be
an object for identification by audiences thousands of miles away. In
the place of that particular smell, those remote people can posit the
odour of hot chocolate, of a squashed banana in their kindergarten
of long ago, or of a different grass growing where they live. From an
emotional point of view, therefore, the identification with different
sense data can nonetheless easily create the impression that the playwright was trying to make. Furthermore, regionalism or "localism"
can be considered a radical rather than reactionary approach to
drama, as a creative, authentic force, not only in Canada but also
in New Zealand, Israel or many countries in the third world, that
are beginning to shape their identity through theatre.

The borders between the local and the universal are gradually
becoming blurred; international theatre festivals take place all over
the world, television is widespread, and a great variety of plays are
available through which people may encounter non-local drama.
A look at the entertainment supplements of Canadian and Israeli
newspapers (and in fact those of any big city in the world) may provide an indication not only of the number of theatrical performances
in relation to the population of one particular city or another, but
also of the relationship between stage supply and audience demand,
the degree of artistry or commercialism of the entire theatrical
profile, and of the repertoire during one season or another. Further
scanning would show the relationship between theatre productions
and television programmes, radio, sport, movies, music, etc. in any
given city.

London's West End, the Mecca of the well-made professional
English theatre, is a touristic theatrical attraction, satisfying the real
or imaginary cultural thirst of English speakers and stutterers. West
End plays are often comfortably tailored to a very general taste, as
uninvolved and uncommitted as possible. The same often applies
to Broadway musicals, catering to the lowest common denominator
of entertainment, focusing mostly on local people's pocket and
American taste. Taking real artistic chances through ideological

or political commitment is fairly rare in such plays, since in doing
so the producer may lose a considerable number of ticket sales.
In London, Toronto, Tel Aviv and New York, one can always
rely on the existence of "professional," "entertaining," "showy"
productions, which excel in providing a low-calorie diet as regards
genuine artistic content. A critic such as Anton Wagner talks about
the Canadian productions of *Cats* or *Tamara*, and the epic opera *Ra*,
which at least is really Canadian.[3] Similarly, the Tel Aviv Cameri
theatre production of *Les Misérables* received enthusiastic reviews
and the Israeli singer–cantor who played the lead was even granted
an audience with Queen Elizabeth. In Bangkok live about six and a
half million people, who enjoy (or suffer from) far less theatre, local,
universal or even musical, than the inhabitants of Jerusalem, who
number about a quarter of a million. The average repertoire in Oak-
land and Wellington in New Zealand, Vancouver and Edmonton in
Canada, Strasbourg and Metz in France, includes a few classicals
by Shakespeare and Molière and some plays by Chekhov, Ibsen
and Shaw, as well as modern plays dealing, moderately, with
social and economic problems, woman's rights, ethnic or sexual
minorities, cancer patients and criminals and so on. In these places
one also finds many musical comedies, which play to good houses
and sometimes subsidize the more artistically ambitious and risky
productions of larger theatres. The choice of repertoire depends on
the country's cultural background and on the existence of theatrical
traditions and government support, as can clearly be seen in the case
of the well-subsidized modern German theatre, which hardly needs
to depend on the money coming in from the audience.

Scanning these entertainment sections may provide an impression
of the relationship between original and imported plays. What kind
of a reaction can one expect from an audience seeing *Rosenkrantz
and Guildenstern are Dead* by Stoppard, without their knowing
Shakespeare's *Hamlet*? What would a Jerusalem academic audience
of European background obtain from a reconstruction of a play by
the Egyptian Ahmad Shuki called *Majnun's Laila*, performed by
a group of Jewish actors from Iraq? The Prague *Laterna Magica*
company managed to convey highly charged political messages
before December 1989, yet their 1991 production of *Odysseus* is a
slick, generalized and non-committed pseudo quest-play. Is *Waiting
for Godot* indeed a universal play, because it is not located under
the bridges of the Seine in Paris, or somewhere around the Liffy in
Dublin, or anywhere between the Yarkon and Ben Yehuda bridges

in Tel Aviv? Or perhaps along the St. Lawrence, under the Cartier bridge in Montreal? What happens (and happens very well) to Chekhov's plays in England? Or in France? To Peter Brook's special production of *The Cherry Orchard*, or to certain rather boring contemporary productions of Chekhov by Russian theatres? What happens to Molière in Japan; to Euripides' *Medea*, shown in Kabuki style at the Israel festival, or to a play on the Holocaust by the Israeli playwright Yehoshua Sobol, shown in Germany? In New York? In London? – receiving excellent reviews for very different reasons in each of these respective cities.

A Night in May, an Israeli play that will be more thoroughly examined later on, was produced in Montreal in 1974, and was not particularly successful. In 1988 a mini festival of Canadian drama took place at the theatre department of Tel Aviv University, where *The Crackwalker* by Judith Thompson and *Blood Relations* by Sharon Pollock were presented, as well as stage readings of *Forever Yours, Mary Lou*, by Tremblay – with considerable artistic success. The Canadian message was carried across, although the commercial response was fairly limited.

As preparation for the discussion of an Israeli and a Canadian play, from the point of view of local and universal, we may first look at a well-known modern classic, apparently very local and yet providing a model for many imitations, combining the local with the universal in a most convincing way: *Riders to the Sea* (1904) by J. M. Synge.[4] From a dramatic point of view, the play is composed like a classical Greek tragedy,[5] dealing with the circumstances of real or imaginary people, and with the destiny of humanity in general, through mental and spiritual archetypes. Synge's *Riders to the Sea* focuses on humanity's war with destiny and nature, with courage, with death and love. But no less effective than the dramatic power of the play, is the subtle, clear and sophisticated usage of offstage.

The play takes place in the kitchen of a fisherman's shack on the small "Island [of Arran], off the West of Ireland" – far from England which is itself separated from Europe, the centre stage of culture. At the outset of the play a man who drowned in Donegal is mentioned by the two sisters Nora and Cathleen and "she herself" (Maurya, an old woman) will go and search by the sea. After the words "'She'll be getting her death,' says he, 'with crying and lamenting'" a gust of wind blows the door open as though the outside is breaking in – a non-verbal theatrical portent of what will tragically and inevitably happen later.

The title, *Riders to the Sea,* from a dramatic point of view and from that of the characters themselves, is an "onstage" name, but from the production and the theatrical point of view, it is typically offstage. Maurya's husband and her six sons all went riding to the sea. Maurya, in a vision which is both insight and reality, Anagnorisis and Peripetiea, sees Bartley, her last surviving son, riding on the red mare. Her description, in the classical spirit, is a look outward (ironic in its context) and at the same time inward. Furthermore, since the people of Arran make their poor living by transporting horses on tiny boats over the stormy, rocky and most dangerous sea, the evocation of the horses functions on the concrete level throughout the play, evoking the actual and realistic world of the characters, as well as on the symbolic and metaphorical level. On the one hand *Riders to the Sea* is a specifically local affair, yet on the other, the pale horse, the grey pony in the play, has many connotations: "and his name was Death" (Revelations 6:8); The horses of Poseidon, the Greek god of the sea; "the horse and his rider hath he thrown into the sea" (Exod. 15:1); Slepnir, Odin's grey horse. Synge was certainly aware of the universal meaning of his image, as becomes clear from some of his explicit comparisons of Irish and Greek mythology.[6]

The sea is most assuredly the main figure, albeit the antagonist. It appears a great deal in the characters' lines, since it is in the sea that they find their sustenance, and their deaths. The sea is a physical entity, a mental and spiritual one from a dramatic point of view, and a constantly threatening presence from a theatrical point of view – an offstage at the same close and distant. Inasmuch as Synge was influenced by Maeterlinck's *Interieur* (1894), by Pierre Loti's *Pecheur d'Islande,* and by Herman Hierman's *Meerspiel, On Hoop van Zegen* (1900),[7] his play, as a modern classic, combining an everyday modern approach with a classical structure and mythological motifs in an exceptionally beautiful balance, was to influence many playwrights to come. Bertolt Brecht, for one, took the main idea of the riders to the sea, and rewrote it as *The Guns of Señora Carrar* (1937). However, Brecht's offstage is no longer the sea but an entity hungry for the lives of people during the Spanish Civil War. He completes the theatrical gap with an explicit political interpretation which was only one of the possible meanings hinted at by Synge.

Pursuing the notion of offstage, one finds other variations on the conflict between the universal and the local in the plays of the

Canadian Michael Cook and A. B. Yehoshua, an Israeli playwright. The specific Jerusalem described by Yehoshua is unfamiliar to the faraway citizens of Newfoundland, as is the fisherman's village in Newfoundland to Jerusalemites, notwithstanding a number of biblical allusions in both plays. Of course the cultural allusion to the Bible works differently on Jewish native speakers of Hebrew and on English speakers of Christian background.

Yehoshua's plays have been accused of a certain amount of literariness, while it was said about Cook that he "has failed . . . to get beneath the surface idiosyncrasies of these people and invest them with a degree of dimension."[8] It is, however, this very literariness, that is, the non-realization in theatrical terms in the case of Yehoshua, who is mainly a novelist, and a certain propensity for melodrama, as ascribed to Cook, which enable an examination of the respective fictional spaces they have created, since such spaces are more clearly revealed in proportion to the gap (lessened in Cook's case and widened in Yehoshua's) between the intentions of the text and the stage actualization.

In both cases one is dealing with playwrights who have chosen to write about local issues in order to harness them to a message extending far beyond the borders of Jerusalem or Newfoundland.

A. B. Yehoshua's *A Night in May* (1969)[9] takes place in Jerusalem. As an ex-Jerusalemite, Yehoshua is very familiar with the streets surrounding the imaginary building around which the events occur. Michael Cook's plays are set in Newfoundland where he has been living, and they too are very local, set in a neighbourhood known intimately only to the inhabitants. In *Head, Guts and Soundbone Dance* (1972)[10] and *Jacob's Wake* (1974)[11] – Cook's best play according to some critics[12] – he deals with problems of survival and adds his voice to the famous Canadian motif. "A man is a small place," says Peter, one of Cook's protagonists; but he lives in a very big place as far as space is concerned, and, with his small size, tries to survive the immensity of surrounding nature. The space around is not seen, but only hinted at on stage; it encircles the individual and his family as a close group. "The sea wanted him," a character says, employing a typical image; yet in the present context one must examine whether the sea is a *dividing* space between onstage and offstage; or an absorbing space, or an oppressive kind of space, directed from the outside inwardly. Concomitantly, we shall look at the kind of space perception found in Yehoshua: the characters are enclosed in one room in a Jerusalem house "to which one descends by six or eight steps" and soon one learns that this room, the only space presented in the play, functions also as a womb, a tomb, and a shelter.

In *Head, Guts and Soundbone Dance*, as the stage directions indicate, the set is located on the verge between the outside and the inside. When the tide rises, water floods the house. In *Jacob's Wake* too, Cook recommends total realism for the set design, although he indicates his acceptance in principle of other possibilities. He asks for a sense of confinement and of increasing claustrophobic suffocation, reinforcing the emotional tensions which grow throughout the play. In both *A Night in May* and *Head, Guts and Soundbone Dance*, the threshold between outside and inside is emphasized in the required stage syntax, which plays a key role in the way the sets function as an image for the meaning of the entire play. The door, and indeed the threshold itself, is halfway between darkness and light, between anxiety and security; and on yet another metaphorical level, between sanity and insanity, between psychological stress and the chances for spiritual and mental redemption. There is a clear intimation in the Canadian play that the outside is "good," whereas in the Hebrew play the outside connotes "danger" and potential evil.

In both plays, the first scene is primarily intended to make the audience aware of the discrepancy between the outside and the inside. From the moment that something starts to happen, something which is more than a static picture of a stage from which the curtain has been withdrawn, a dialogue begins not merely between people but rather between two expressive theatrical modes, the visual and the auditory. At the same time, the realistic image of the play is immediately counteracted.

In Yehoshua's *A Night in May*, the radio emitting voices has no "natural" reason to do so. The first words in this play indeed come from the radio: "And here is the weather forecast." These words will gain their due metaphorical proportion retrospectively, linked not necessarily with the state of the weather, but rather with the state of the atmosphere. With these same "atmospheric" words, which have absorbed added significance throughout the performance, based on information given to the audience, the play also ends. By this time, no one has any illusion that the author was merely discussing the weather.

"A long night. A vast plain. A burning fire": in Israel, these are coded phrases broadcast to call reserve soldiers to report to their units. As voices only, these theatrically transmitted radiophonic words obtain a visual response. A light is turned on over the stairs. In an elegant dialogue Yehoshua counterpoints the weather forecast with the hesitant entry of a character. The hesitation is soon modified by the increasingly urgent action of a ringing doorbell, while the radio is still emitting the temperatures for the following day. The man from the outside enters from the light and the open air into the darkness within. This dialogue transmits a state of tension and conflict also to those who are not involved with that particular Israeli milieu, while those who understand the contents of the message, surely gain an additional level of significance. A translation of this section of the play would not greatly reduce the effect of this opening scene, which is mainly non-verbal.

Tirza, who is sprawling on the couch, responds in a confused way to the door-bell. She reacts first to the radio, and goes to the door only after five peals. The hesitation of the man on the other side of the doorstep is charged with underlying impatience, and speeds up the tempo of the scene. On the edge of darkness and light, a man and a woman meet in an intimate embrace between the inside and the outside, the man in a state of excessive intensity, the woman tired and apathetic.

Although not directly linked with notions of offstage, a further discussion of the opening scene is necessary in order to explain the context in which offstage is used here. "Universal" versus "local" elements are also emphasized. Within a few moments of the beginning of the performance, a dense series of dialogues already exists in this visual–auditory interplay; between the dialogue text and the authorial text, between the lighting and the sets and between two people and moods. This dialogue transmits meaning not only to those familiar with the milieu. The first words spoken by an acted character are also characteristic of the contradiction set up between the content and the expression of what is uttered. "You?" is a question asked only when the answer is known, regardless of language or culture. Avi's response is at first non-verbal: "He bends over her, kisses her eyes." Only later when he answers "Me" do we become aware that he, like Tirza, is speaking on an emotional rather than literal level. It is not unreasonable to assume that the words "kisses her eyes" will be interpreted differently from culture to culture. Even in Israel such tenderness may mean different things to different ethnic groups. But whatever the possible variations, it is universally clear that kissing the eyes is an intimate act. In the course of this play, it is the first hint of a brother–sister relationship which is full of jealousy and suggestive of incest.

Avi answers Tirza's next question "What's happened?" with another question "What time is it?" It is this non-committal answer which reveals that it is Avi who is in control and has the upper hand. Tirza responds to Avi's question about the time but then demands an answer to her original query. She then asks "What in the world are you doing in Jerusalem?" At the precise moment that she asks this, the light in the outside hall goes off, and the first "beat" of the opening scene comes to an abrupt halt. From this point onward the strange affectionate dialogue is carried on in the dark. In the darkness (*qua* offstage on-stage!) we learn about the nature of the two characters' relationship, the forces that propel their actions, and most important, the possibility of the outbreak of war. It is obvious that this dialogue operates on at least two levels simultaneously. For besides hearing a conversation that is untypical of two siblings who have not seen each other for some time, one also observes that the two react not to what has been said but to the sub-textual meaning of the words:

> *Avi*:   My generation is past fighting anyhow.
> *Tirza*:   You're shivering though.

Tirza responds to Avi's physical behavior in the embrace, not to the words he speaks. In this exchange, both Tirza's vulnerability and Avi's nervousness are dramatized. Avi reacts as strongly to the sub-textual meaning as his sister:

> *Avi*:   . . . But – who are you hiding from in the dark?
> *Tirza*:   I'm not hiding . . .

The obsessiveness of Avi's nature, which is hinted at when he repeatedly rings the doorbell and asks about the time, is fully illustrated in his continual evasion of his sister's questions. Later, he "takes revenge" for the fact that she can see past his exterior and into his true self. Although he embraces her, he does not cross the threshold of the door, which symbolically is the point where the bright outside meets the sombre inside world. At this moment the audience witnesses the fundamental elements of production and the basic modes of theatrical expression at work. The lighting becomes alive and the movement very defined. Avi becomes nervous and agitated while Tirza, on the other hand, becomes slower, sleepier, and more quiet. Even the turning on of the radio is deliberate, aimed at illuminating more of the meaning of this first expositional scene.

As the play progresses it becomes evident that the external dramatic action is minimalistic, being only an echo of the emotional activity that is going on inside the main characters (the family situation is complicated). Here objects behave as words while words sometimes descend to the level of objects. (It is not coincidental that Yehoshua entitled another play of his *Things*.)

In *The Head, Guts and Soundbone Dance*, too, things happen before the first words are uttered, and there too the set is meant to "speak." Whereas *A Night in May* opens in the evening and ends in the morning, the Newfoundland play starts at early dawn and ends at dusk, when a light enters from the "church window." This window is an interpretative option, hovering as a reminder of what can be said about "redemption" should the playwright think fit. Pete finds a lantern and lights it.

With the early morning light, a faint sound of the sea is heard. Skipper Pete goes to the door but does not yet open it, in the same way that Avi hesitates before ringing the doorbell at the house where he once lived. Pete stands listening and immediately seagulls are heard, and the wind blows the door open towards him. The outside, no doubt, needs fortification from the inside, and Pete indeed fixes the door, thus drawing attention to the metaphoric discrepancy between the in and the outside. He glances outside, urinates, returns and organizes the inside for himself by lighting the fire. Uncle John enters after the song, bringing with him both weather and atmosphere.

In *Jacob's Wake*, all seven participants, as in *A Night in May*, are three generations of one family. Here Michael Cook requires the storm outside to become "a living thing, a character whose presence is always felt if not actually heard on stage."[13] The design of the interior is supposed to be as natural as possible, contrasting in its warmth with the cold outside. This meticulous attention to realistic detail will later enhance the progress towards the abstract and the symbolic. Rosie is revealed on stage sewing; Mary is correcting schoolwork. Both women carry on an indirect, non-verbal dialogue with each other and both together have a "dialogue" with the gusts of wind outside. The first words here, as in *The Head, Guts and Soundbone Dance* and *A Night in May* are very important: "I just can't do any more"; "God damn door"; "You?" These opening lines act as epigraphs for all three plays, in all of which the man enters from the outside and the woman is already within.

In *Jacob's Wake* too, the sound of the radio is an active voice introducing "another" world, exclusively vocal, into the visually present world on the stage. It is not only the actual penetration of the radio into the world of the characters that is important, but also the content of the broadcast, which enhances the tension between the chance of a radiophonic solution and the feeling of "no exit" which accumulates throughout the performance. In *A Night in May*, Yehoshua uses the radio not only in order to insert mobilization signals, later to become images far above and beyond the specific war that broke out in 1967 in the Middle East, but also as a vocal effect very similar to the one used by Cook.

Yehoshua's Israeli specificity is contained not only in his characters, sets and period but also in his sound effects. The voices of the radio announcers and readers of the Bible and the Qur'an all "speak" differently to Israelis than to foreigners. In Israel, the electronic time-signal beeps before to the news immediately conjure up images of anxiety and danger. In times of war, people have been known to guess in advance what the speaker is about to report merely by listening to the tone of the introductory words: "This is Kol Yisrael from Jerusalem with the news read by . . . " The recognition pattern regarding listening to the radio must surely differ for a black in the Bronx carrying a huge transistor radio, and, for example, an Albanian citizen listening to some radio broadcast from the West. Yehoshua also uses particularly local associations and connotations, such as a psalm of Asaph heard over the radio, Asaph being the name of a character in *A Night in May*, a Temple singer, and of an early medieval Jewish doctor.

In *The Head, Guts and Soundbone Dance* the outside "invites" the figures to join it, because of the child the two men have decided not to help. Uncle John goes out, while Pete checks the fire, the fish, re-fixes the door, starts to sing, fills his plate and starts eating. *Jacob's Wake*, on the other hand, ends with a "bang," described as a cosmic catastrophe,[14] and a huge flash of lightning illuminates the stage in a theatrical "freeze," followed by darkness. A moment later the characters have simply vanished. Only the death mask will be lit from within, when inside and outside emerge, vocally and visually, to the quiet howling of a bitter wind. In *A Night in May*, after a long Chekhov-like series of partings and leave-takings, Tirza also goes out and the stage-room remains completely empty, only the radio repeating: "Closed door, long night, huge expanse, burning fire."[15] Dramatically, these two endings are very similar in their apocalyptic ramifications.

Cook and Yehoshua wish to achieve "the naked human situation,"[16] and they try to do so because and sometimes in spite of the specific Canadian or Israeli circumstances from which, through which and especially for which they have written their plays. In *A Night in May* as well as in *Jacob's Wake* the personal and cultural idiosyncracies of the dramatic personae endow the content with credibility not only among audiences well-versed in the culture, but also for complete strangers.

A Night in May maintains a balance between the specifically Israeli milieu and the much more general mental and human one. Here Yehoshua examines his own mental, artistic, inner authenticity, in the context of social and political conditions. These two sorts of authenticity are weighed against each other while the playwright makes life quite difficult for himself. He allows them to clash under controlled stage conditions, knowing quite well that theatre favours the local and the specific.

The universality and specificity of Yehoshua's characters may be approached through Ibsen's onion in *Peer Gynt*. Is Israeliness an onion that peels away, or does it present a garlic-like core? Is there anything specifically Israeli left, once we peel off the layers of time, set, milieu: a specific street in a Jerusalem neighbourhood or a specific period just prior to the Six Day War. Yehoshua has said that "war is a severe anxiety which acts like a catalyst for the outbreak of deeper spiritual crises."[17] But does a "naked self" really exist? Yehoshua dramatizes the question by having his characters, with varying degrees of consciousness, attempt to discard their outer wrappings and arrive at the core. The characters in search of their naked selves use Jewish culture, the State of Israel, Jerusalem under the foreboding of siege, their home, their neighborhood and the thin line between sanity and madness to define who and what they are. Forming a concentric focus to ever widening (or narrowing) ripples of significance, these, within a theatrical context, are the very layers that the characters are asked to shed. By the same token, what would remain if one peels away Canadian Newfoundland skipper Pete's characteristic traits – hat, language, fish, and the weather.

Could he exist without a North American, Canadian, Newfound-land fisherman rind? Although Yehoshua often tends to favour the psychoanalytic interpretation, in *A Night in May* he aspires to something spiritual. We discover an extrapolation whereby the universal becomes more universal in comparison with other works by this writer, and the local becomes yet more specific. The result is a blend of mythic, thematic and erotic tendencies combined with uniquely Israeli details and flavours.

Cook tries to write classical tragedy.[18] Many critics have noted the universal qualities of his plays: Wasserman indicates the harsh existentialism and the apocalyptic ending;[19] Perkyns emphasizes the alienated connection existing in the play between man and his environment;[20] and others refer to "absurd" undertones, especially in *The Head, Guts and Soundbone Dance.*

In both of Cook's sea plays, and in Yehoshua's "land" Jerusalem play, family is the meeting point. The characters are related to each other by blood or marriage. Using the family circle in a play is a strategy that the ancient Greeks, the French neo-classicists, and the protagonists of the Japanese No Theatre all capitalized on in order to heighten the intensity of their drama: emotions of love and hate explode more effectively in family situations than anywhere else. Yehoshua too makes use of this strategy, since family tension is universal.

Other than the family figures appearing in the Canadian and Israeli plays, there are also offstage figures. In *A Night in May,* Tirza's baby is often mentioned; a baby born three months before the play opened, and whom no one in the family wants to see; neither Uncle Avinoam nor ex-husband Amikam and not even Asaph, the doctor, his father. Offstage babies and children have spent many long hours onstage. Bobick is brought on stage in an empty(?) carriage in Chekhov's *The Three Sisters.* In Bond's *Help,* a baby is murdered, and in Beckett's *Endgame,* a child is not allowed on stage. Cook, in a bloodcurdling scene in *Head, Guts and Soundbone Dance* mentions a drowned child in the past, while in the present tense of the performance the two men talking do not reach out a hand to a child who is drowning *now.* The scene evokes Maurya's monologue in *Riders to the Sea* about past funerals, spoken while Bartley's drowned body is being carried home on a plank. In *Jacob's Wake,* another baby is killed on the ice, and skipper Blackborne's son, who is the Jacob of the play's title, also freezes to death. With him, as the biblical allusion makes clear, the entire dynasty is frozen and no twelve tribes will ever be born. The son who continues the family line in *Head, Guts and Soundbone Dance* is mourned for like King David mourning his rebellious son Absalom, and he is a retarded person who draws out the drowned child instead of a fish. In all three plays, the old people are dominant and through them the playwrights extinguish any hope for the future. This is symbolized, in various degrees of sophistication, through the many dead children in the plays. The past holds on fast but is doomed to vanish and the future is murdered. In *A Night in May* some of the figures will go out to war; not many will return. In fact, all the figures expect to die soon one way or another.

Offstage is not only a different space but it may also connote different plots in different times. In Cook's two plays, offstage inhabits the same space but in a different time which the characters prefer to their present fictional time. Some of the people in *A Night in May* also live in an unclear, fantastic past, whether invented or realistic. A different mode of working with time is achieved through locating *A Night in May* between the 22nd and the 23rd of May in 1967, the date on which the Egyptians declared the Straits of Tiran closed to Israeli ships. This, in fact, was the "casus belli" for the outbreak of the Six Day War. Cook sets his play on the Thursday and Friday of Easter; an implied hope for redemption which will fail throughout the performance and enhance the profound disappointment.

Another device to place previous plots in relation to a present temporal spatial stage, is allusion in general and biblical illusion in particular. The use Cook and Yehoshua make of names, for instance, is highly revealing. In Hebrew there is a traditional sensitivity to names that express desires and qualities. Naomi derives from "Noam," pleasantness, Levine from the Levites in the temple, Sarid is the name of the old mother, from a root directly connoting survival, whereas Rachel evokes the verse about a mother who refuses to be consoled for the death of her sons. Rachel is the name of a figure in both *A Night in May and The Head, Guts and Soundbone Dance* – for similar reasons. Peter and John are names of Christ's disciples. All these names play subtle dialogues in which they interpret themselves according to the Bible, and, to a certain extent, interpret the Bible according to themselves. Furthermore, in *A Night in May*, the atrocities comitted against European Jewry are evoked, and in Cook's plays the past glory of Newfoundland is depicted, with a rejection of the present and the destruction of the future. The main characters enclose themselves in their private time–space through feeling besieged in some imaginary biblical space.

This "sealing off" is particularly prominent because the stage activity of most of the figures recalls Chekhov's plays: trivial actions, ritualistically empty and bereft of movement towards actual change, unlike the direction of classical drama. In *A Night in May* they are always preparing coffee which they never drink, while in *The Head, Guts and Soundbone Dance* they clean fish, prepare drinks and build fires. The petty onstage activity is dwarfed by the sounds of the sea, the cries of the seagull, the funeral bells for Aunt Alice and the tumult of bringing in the murdered corpse of a child. In the Israeli play the external radio voices and the gradual vanishing of the characters are dominant and portend war. Elijah (Blackborne) in *Jacob's Wake*, as his name connotes, vanishes in the storm, perhaps not towards heaven because he is a pantheist, but he does indeed evaporate in a streak of lightning, leaving behind him the bitter howl of an offstage wind.[21]

Still in *Jacob's Wake*, Skipper's madness and Rachel's insanity can be seen on a different plane: that of people who inhabit their own stories. However, it is important to realize that it is through the insane insights of Rachel, about to be hospitalized, that one learns about things. She is more lucid than most of the characters in the play. Skipper will retreat to his inner space from the notion of hospitalization and Pete seems to understand the sea only when he is no longer sailing on it. In this sense insanity is a metonymy of the relationship between stage and offstage. The Danse Macabre in *The Head, Guts and Soundbone Dance* functions equally as offstage relating to "plot," which is either inner or external, all depending on the point of view. It is an appeal to another reality, exemplified in *A Night in May* by a long series of recounted dreams as an exposition of an inner offstage which is inside the characters and drawn onto the stage from within rather than without.

Both Yehoshua and Cook have written plays with a considerable amount of specificity. Only those who have grown up in the Jerusalem quarter of Rehavia could actually identify the two trees mentioned in Noa's dream – they are still there. Certainly, Newfoundlanders could also identify particular fishermen's wharfs if they too are still standing. The authors see no real problem in combining the realistic and the symbolic, especially since such a combination belongs to the very core of theatre. Both jump between places, times and offstage plots as a function of changing states of consciousness and attempts to exploit the medium of theatre to broaden awareness. The local element is often a safety device. It is always flesh, a body, a costume, and every now and then some spirit emanates from the mask. To the question "what is local, what is universal?" in *A Night in May*, one can answer that the performance itself is both a dialogue and an invitation to a dialogue. Although it is easier to speak Hebrew to Israelis and a Newfoundland jargon dialect to inhabitants of that area, one can also claim about Cook that the distance between Newfoundland and Jerusalem may sometimes be shorter than that to Ottawa or Montreal (as is clear from the unfavourable reviews he received there).

The main expressive means permitting the closing of the gap between the dramatic or literary, local and universal concepts, is the theatrical relation activated in every performance between the stage and the offstage. On the stage, as is clear from Cook's and Yehoshua's plays, one finds mostly the local characterization. Offstage, as ever growing concentric ripples, we find the universal, penetrating into the individual spectator's mind.

The difference between *Jacob's Wake* and *The Head, Guts and Soundbone Dance* on the one hand, and *A Night in May* on the other, is almost unbridgeable if seen from the local aspect only. The Canadian plays deal with the disintegration of people in a harsh environment, a cold and hostile climate, destroyed by the failure of nostalgia to compensate for their distress, and the shift from a moralist organic society to an alienated urban one. *A Night in May* documents some Israelis' fears of a war that has yet to break out in the play, but in non-theatrical reality, has already happened. They use the premonition of war as a pretext to liberate them from the real commitment to themselves and to their fellows, especially their family. In these plays, the psychological, social, ideological and universal aspects are harnessed to unique modes of very local presentation. The heroes are fighting for their sanity, identity, lives and deaths. In the meantime, their behaviour is highly destructive.

Since the sea usually remains offstage as an image of eternity, of the elements of nature and of war, the characters in the Canadian and Israeli plays all ride to the universal sea on local horses. It is the specific Israeliness or Canadianness of these works that makes it possible for them to be performed outside their native countries. As an exercise in theatricality it might be interesting to perform *The Head, Guts and Soundbone Dance* on the set design originally meant for *A Night in May* and vice versa. One thing remains beyond doubt, however: in these three plays by Cook and Yehoshua, offstage, on the threshold of which the plot "takes place," has the upper hand and its victory is determinant and fatal. The universal human element in all plays thus proves stronger than the local and indigenous.

3

Mythical Space, Pathos and Irony

Whereas the discussion in the previous chapter dealt with both local and universal elements, here I will treat a topic which might appear to be entirely local – the earth and the relationship to it; although, naturally, the very tendency to deal with the earth is in itself universal. In considering the need to find a connection with the earth, and with newly-acquired space, we shall examine how Canadians and Israelis relate to their own piece of land, sometimes with a touch of pathos, and sometimes ironically.

With the crystallization of European nationalism from the middle of the nineteenth century onward, many national movements drew on their supposedly glorious past, on folklore and on ancient myths, for support. The independence of Greece, the unification of Spain, Poland, Italy and Germany, were all greatly encouraged by the ideological relationships set up between blood, man and earth. In Hebrew, these three words stem from one etymological root (Heb.: "dam," "adam," "adama"). From an historical point of view, sometimes concretized through political manipulation, the ties between peoples and territories were redefined and the earth itself was, became, or was declared to be, holy; even though with varying doses of precision and psychological, social, political, and spiritual authenticity.

German romanticism hailed the connection with the earth.[1] Yeats quotes old Irish poetry and talks about "the holy land of Ireland." In Russia, Tolstoy's last years were dedicated to mystical attempts to renew the connection with the earth through a close association with the "Narodnik" (The People) movement. Earth literature is reflected in the contents and even the names of works such as *The Bliss of the Earth* by Knut Hamsun, *The New Earth* by Harwood, *The Good Earth* by Pearl S. Buck, *The Earth* by Emil Zola, and *Virgin Earth* (or land) by Sholokhov. After the October revolution, a "social-realistic" mythization developed, Marxist materialistic in declaration, but no less mythological in character than romanticism, proclaiming the spiritual links between man, toil, and earth.

The connection between national revival and the earth can be seen in the arts of painting, sculpture and theatre in both Canada[2] and Israel, two countries whose full political and national independence was achieved after World War II, even though in different circumstances. Given two typical immigration countries, one can discern in Hebrew and Canadian drama of the last decades a deliberate tendency towards depicting the uniqueness of the geographic and historical space as part of a conscious and political effort to shape nationalism. Within the attempts at local modes of shaping, especially in the first years of the creation of drama, it is evident that the land, the country, the very soil, nature, the fields, agriculture, all perform a most important role.

People who feel secure with their land and nationality, an issue depending also on the historical background, require much less strengthening of their relationship to the earth than people in the midst of a process of becoming. Such a process always suffers from a considerable amount of insecurity, especially among immigrants, among people under foreign rule, and in new nations where art is very often harnessed to the nation-moulding effort. Mobilization can be satiric, or contain the pathos of government-directed ideological channeling; but, more often than not, these two tendencies are complementary.

In relatively stable, independent countries, which people leave rather than enter, such as France and England over the last few hundred years, it is harder to find drama sanctifying the earth. On the other hand, Sean O'Casey, in *The Plough and the Stars*, quite naturally presents the connection between the Irish people and their land, since land was a major issue in the Anglo-Irish conflict. Chekhov depicts the division between Russians and their land in *The Cherry Orchard*, but in the revolutionary propaganda productions of the play not too many years later, an effort was made to adapt the severed connection, if not to the land itself, at least to the need of production from it. In the same way we find Soviet plays, posters and dances about ploughs and tractors, and choirs and dramas about factory production lines. This direction was certainly influenced by futuristic aesthetics, as expressed in the manifestos of Marinetti, Mayakovski and various expressionist trends. In Germany, before unification in 1870, we occasionally find "earth" oriented plays. In the agit-prop skits of the twenties[3] and in the plays of the Third Reich, the link between blood and the land was strongly emphasized, whether in the spirit of Nietzsche's *Thus Spake Zarathustra*, which was politically misinterpreted as "keep allegiance to the land," or in a more extreme way, with a typical nationalistic blend of kitsch and death.[4] This "spirit of the earth," known from the plays of Goethe and Wedekind, for instance, became in fascist drama a sweet and somber propagandistic element. And again, in Brecht's *The Caucasian Chalk Circle*, the main metaphor of the play is very clear. Land belongs to whoever works on it, rather than to those who just happen to own it.

Australian Aborigines, from a totally different point of view, believe in the sanctity of the land, but at the same time, and perhaps for that same reason, nobody *owns* it. The same is true for the Bedouin in some of the Arab countries and in present-day Israel. The settled Palestinian population, on the other hand, has always had a strong and locally-specific attachment to its lands.[5] American Indians, or some of them, also had a sacerdotal attitude towards the earth. Lacking an exclusivistic sense of ownership until forced to react to political deprivation by the internalization of European sensitivities and ideologies, the Red Indians, like the Aborigines, are claiming ownership of the land.

Under the influence of romanticism and nationalism on the one hand and various sorts of socialism on the other, together with the emergence of new theatrical trends and playwrights, "earth-oriented" plays have been written in both Canada and Israel. In the early years they were drenched in pathos, but a generation or two later a more tacit acceptance of nationalism by second or third generation immigrants can be sensed. The "element of earth," with many playwrights, becomes material for a satirical, ironical, sober and much more critical but not less loving, approach.

Throughout the years of the first arrivals of immigrants Hebrew literature overflowed with notions of earth. During some 1800 years of exile, after the destruction of the Second Temple in 70 AD, a few Jews went on living in the land of Israel. There, as well as in the many diasporas, some were farmers, yet most of the Jewish people had no actual contact with the earth, or with agriculture and nature in general, and were cut off from their pre-exilic land. The sharp transition of the early Jewish pioneers from central and eastern European cities and townlets to the desert, the heat, the swamps and the mosquitoes of Palestine, was part of the deliberate effort of those few tens of thousands of people to transform their lives according to their pioneering ideology: no more dependency, minor trading, artisanship in exile and diaspora; but a "home-coming" to the land of the patriarchs and a fulfilled yearning for a renewed link between the people, the land and the culture. The Jewish religion, under historical necessity, had exchanged the territorial national circumstances of the biblical Hebrew kingdom for the various diasporas and the holy books. Study of the Torah and the legal code became a "territory," highly spiritual, but for all that, also very concrete. With a renewed merging with the fatherland, it also became necessary to return to the land itself. Exile, as A. D. Gordon, one of the leading ideologues, declared,

> ... is an unnatural form of national life, and people need a real connection with the fields and nature. As long as man comes in direct contact with the elements of nature, living according to its rhythm and does not create for himself a secluded realm of human life, closed within itself, he does indeed add from his special human power to nature in the direction of the flowing meant for man, and he lives life as a direct continuation of nature.[6]

The mystical, cosmic dimension of Gordon's attitude suggests a way towards development and wholeness, where man can find the satisfaction of continual progress.

This return to the homeland occurred in the midst of a social and personal identity crisis for many Jews. Zionism, which in those years shortly before the first World War, was beginning to be transformed from a religious yearning into a national and social movement, needed the tangible land as a real solution for the adversities of the Jewish people, and it thus idealized the soil itself. From a personal point of view, many of the pioneers carried with them the difficulties of parting from their families, of severing themselves from their old countries and cultures, together with the desire to heal their bodies, souls and spirits in the rebirth of the land of Israel. The dialectic link with the soil in those years was often compatible with a non-materialistic attitude to life and with typically spiritual inclinations. More often than not the pioneers relinquished bourgeois comfort in the search for their inner being. It is not by chance that much Hebrew drama from the twenties to the present day deals with the myths of the second wave of immigration, those founding fathers who built the first kibbutzim. The twenties' pioneers combined group dynamics, psychoanalysis and Marxism, and liberated sex with immense yearnings for a better world, a better society and a better self. As the great "isms" offered by Communism in Russia and nationalism and liberalism in Europe proved disappointing to Jews, many of whom were highly idealistic as well as secular in their attitude to life, only one option remained – Palestine; at least as far as they themselves were concerned.

The play *Earth* by "Shin" Shalom[7] describes a sort of "New Testament" and one must emphasize the revolution occurring in a traditional Jew to make him present his play in such a Christian association, and even introduce a definite erotic contact between the pioneers and their land. "A new settlement we shall build here, and we shall call its name here in Israel 'Adama' (Earth). It will be as an everlasting testimony that the people of Israel has returned from its exile wanderings, from its castles in the air, and come back to its source, to mother earth, to work and to guard . . . "[8]

Gideon Ofrat, in his book on the ritual of earth in Hebrew drama, enumerates dozens of works filled with motifs of earth and land. He too notices the symbolism of "neglecting an imaginary phallus for the benefit of a primary womb." The "womb" element, often identified with the earth, may offer a solution for those immigrant pioneers, who have lost their primal confidence on leaving their former "mother" country. One can thus interpret the yearning for the earth from historical, psychoanalytic or Marxist points of view, but in this context we shall emphasize the modes of relating to the earth as to a theatrical space.

It seems natural that in many Israeli plays, like *Allah Karim, Tents in the Wind, Earth* and others, the key scenes should take place not within walls, but apparently in the outdoors, on the land of some kibbutz. Only later does one observe that the siege consciousness imported from the ghetto and reinforced by the need for barriers against the Arab inhabitants of the country has not vanished but has been only temporarily pushed aside. It is interesting to note that the small size of the country did not prevent these early playwrights from experiencing and describing it in terms of yearning for "open" spaces rather than closed ones. Enclosure as a dominant motif ensued later on from an internalization of the feeling of being besieged rather than from an actual attitude to nature. To people emerging from East European towns, the emptiness of the country, as it was perceived then, was a great openness. Nevertheless, already in the twenties and thirties, one can find the "siege consciousness" expressed in many stage designs as a closed space, defended by and defending the characters; while another dominant line goes on testifying to the sense of open space, long distances and free air. The balance between the closed and the open is that achieved between the inner besieged space that the pioneers brought with them from their East European origins, and the Mediterranean skies, the nature, and the land of Palestine. This also led to a particular perception of stage space, and indeed, scenery designed in accordance with a world view.[9]

The orchard, the vineyard and the field are the fruit of man's intercourse with nature. In Hebrew drama (a similar phenomenon is also found in poetry and prose), many stage occurrences are set either in intensively farmed agricultural areas, in irrigated fields, or against a rocky landscape that needs ploughing and fertilizing, or naturally watered fields which can be considered as wilder and less domesticated. This is a treatment of both stage and natural space which is undergoing cultivation, human investment and involvement. One of the best well-known and enduring of Israeli myths is that of planting trees. Trees are planted not only to afforest a region, and improve the climate, but also, and explicitly so, to send roots down into the earth and achieve stability in an actual physical way. "The soil itself demands victims. We have no other way but to occupy a piece of totally dejected land, be it even swamp land and conquer it with our blood. We shall achieve nothing without great sacrifice."[10] But also, "in the orchard . . . a constant movement, a rhythm of work, of talking, of laughing and chanting with a blend of brother, man and mother earth, a communion with the entire creation."[11]

Immediately after the war of independence in 1948, three plays were staged that clearly signified the beginning of the Israeli rather than the Hebrew Land of Israel oriented drama. In each of these we find an interesting metamorphosis of the motif of earth and land. In *He Walked in the Fields,* by Moshe Shamir (1948), the very name is significant in much the same way as that of the Canadian *Of the Fields Lately.* The image of Uri, the "Sabra" (i.e. a Jew born in the country), is of one who sheds his blood, a sacrifice to the houses and fields of the kibbutz, and indeed, to the whole land. The entire play is depicted in flashback, thrusting towards some imaginary future. It is the evening of Uri's memorial day, twenty years after his death in the fighting, opening with the words "Where is the iron? . . . No, without iron it will not ring. Once there was iron here . . . There should be a piece of iron now . . . There was a time when you could have found a piece of iron here in the yard, a plough, a pipe, a hoe. Today it's clean. Grass lawns . . . lovely, really lovely. But the iron is gone . . . "[12] Shamir here foretells a nostalgia for the strange blend of weapons and farming tools, ploughshares and spears, as he imagines a cultivated landscape, the grass lawns of the kibbutz, twenty years after Uri has given his life to make this possible. The technique of *He Walked in the Fields* is reminiscent of Canadian plays of a docu-dramatic nature, in which one can also find many allusions earth myths, and a dramatization of bits and pieces in a collage style, such as *The Farmer's Revolt, Riel, The Donelleys*, and *The Farm Show*, which deliberately ignore the consecutive sequences of time, space and plot. It is the spectator who is expected to synthesize the components; invited by the author to be more involved and more committed. The protagonist of the play thus grows larger than life and greater than the reality that gave him birth, since he lives simultaneously in different times and spaces. Riel, the eponymous hero of the play, like Uri, achieves strength because the classical convention of the unity of space is ignored and the space of the protagonist becomes an offstage characterized by its half-way situation between ritual and image, symbol and myth.

When an infant drama tries to confront problems of identity and create national heroes, it is often helped not only by deliberately delineating the local landscape, but also by blurring it: the details of the scenery are anyway well known to performers and audiences. In both Israeli and Canadian drama the realistic approach to design testifies to the attempt to show the audience its life-like reflection from the stage, thus harnessing the theatre to the struggle for national identity. But the same effect can be achieved in a more sophisticated way by transmitting to the audience an offstage space with an almost mystical, supernatural character. A reverse device is used by the Theatre Passe Muraille in *Farm Show*. They draw the map of the area where they are performing on the floor of the stage, to reflect the farmers' own image, adding the names of real neighbouring farms. Here we find the same apparatus of mythization in its demystificatory phase. Other plays try to draw a portrait of the collective values of an entire community, or of a particular type and a characteristic hero, using swift transitions, a collage of speakers, and moving from the highly specific to the very general.

In *The Wastes of the Negev* (the southern desert part of Israel) by Yigal Mosenson (1949), one of the space formulations most typical of Israeli drama is revealed; the Bunker, the local version of the Canadian Garrison. That second year of the war of independence marked a clear modification of the yearning for the "open" and wide land which had been relatively predominant in previous years. Now the earth can be seen performing an additional function, being used for trenches and other defensive structures. The main issue presented in the play is whether to abandon the kibbutz under the pressure of the Egyptian siege and leave the land, or to continue to sacrifice human lives and cleave to the settlement as well as to the holy land. A character also says "And I tell you that if we shall have fig leaves and olive leaves on our shoulders and not in our orchards, this will not be a state."[13] Olive and fig leaves are the insignia of officers in the Israeli army. Although the writer offers an alternative ideology, the stage rhetoric of the play connotes a clear feeling for the sanctity of the land.

In *They 'll Arrive Tomorrow*, set in a specific period of the War of Independence, and a more interesting and profound work than the two previous ones, Nathan Shaham describes a company of soldiers stuck on a hill where seven mines have been buried, and the map locating them has been lost. The mines become a metaphorical focus for deteriorating human relationships, for the unravelling of fraternity among brothers in arms, and for an exploitative attitude towards the Arabs. Finally, and this may not have been the playwright's original intention, the mines hint at the dangerous possibility that the earth itself, if overly sanctified, can become lethally explosive.[14]

He Walked in the Fields takes place in a kibbutz under siege, and *The Wastes of the Negev* mostly in the trenches of a kibbutz, while *They 'll Arrive Tomorrow* views the exploding mines from the inside of a semi-destroyed Arab house which serves as the headquarters for the company's officers. The structure of these three plays, examples of many more of the same kind, reflects physical suffocation, enclosure and claustrophobia.

Dianne Bessai's postscript to a collection of Canadian prairie plays could equally well be applied to quite a number of Israeli plays: "Most of the drama specifically created for these theatres, both past and present, falls into regional, thematic patterns, most probably because the dramatization of a localized consciousness and localized action has seemed the most accessible route to a grass root audience."[15] Bessai's words could have been inserted in the printed program of *The Wastes of the Negev,* had they been written in Tel Aviv in 1949.

In Bessai's collection it is interesting to examine the locations established by the playwrights. *Breaches from Bond Street* by Elsie Park Gowen offers the space of a backyard in a southern Alberta hotel, suggesting that the play takes place on the verge between the in and the outside, close to a new fence and a gate. The play ends with the words "Always hope, in the West, if we got the spirit in us," and with pouring a bucket of water on Charlie's head. The stage directions mention little trees that want to grow. Above the fence, as a poetic instruction, are "blue Alberta skies."

In *Broken Globe* the frame of a screen door is emphasized and the play ends with the words "Look out there. Where the earth touches the sky. She is that." And again, in the stage direction, people stand looking *out.* In *A Fine Colored Easter Egg* by Gwen Farris Ringwood a yard is again described as well as the interior of Georgia's hut on the prairie in northern Alberta. There is no call for realism, but here again the close connection between inside and outside is made clear, and Ringwood asks that the separate activities of both realms should be well defined. In Joanna Glass's play *Canadian Gothic,* there are three suggested chairs and a window frame hanging in the air. At the end of the text the dramatic personae are required to close the windows, but since there is no explicit direction for them to do so, they remain open. In *Wheat City,* by Ken Mitchell, the dramatic action takes place on a loading platform in a railway station, immediately suggesting vast expanses. The train comes from somewhere and will keep on going somewhere else. The railway station itself is in a state of slow dilapidation. The distance remains but the access to it is reduced. In the final monologue Rose says "And – maybe sometime – I kin come and see yer – meteor station (. . .) We're the last people in Wheat City!" She too stands at the end looking to her right with a mixture of hope and disappointment, as the stage darkens. In *Seeds,* by Gordon Pengili, we are taken inside the inner space of a kitchen in southern Alberta, but from outside come the howling of a dog, the voice of a harmonica, and finally gusts of wind. Memories are being evoked and so the inside space of the characters is united with the many external spaces made present through their recollections.

The consciousness of nature and scenery is prominent in these local plays not only because most of them are located on the threshold between the inside and the outside, but because in most of them we are aware of the infinite size of the space hovering over the storyline and of the feeling of being sucked out beyond at the end even though the character remains in place. The space of real nature that enfolds the play is not only present on stage, but becomes, as a perfectly justified aura, a dominant element. Offstage space, with its physical and spiritual strength, is an active partner in these plays; since many of them were produced "on location," the geographical surroundings became actual as well as dramatic offstage space. The more the inhabitants of the prairies, of the Israeli Negev, or of any similar region in the world, feel themselves isolated, the more their plays too tend to be "earthy" as an image of clinging to the landscape of their country, whether it be a natural homeland or an acquired one.

It is noticeable that although space is closed off and besieged in the Israeli plays described above, at this stage in the development of Hebrew drama there is still some room for hope outside the confinement. In the Canadian prairie plays, which are no less local, and perhaps subtler in their modes of description than their Israeli counterparts, space is an open area threatening to sweep the people out rather than to squeeze and oppress them.

To examine these two modes of space more specifically, we shall look more closely at two early works: Aharon Ashman's *This Land* (1940) and Herman Voaden's *Hill Land* (1934).

The importance of *Hill Land*,[16] although it is probably unique in Canadian drama, cannot be doubted, Canadian scholars never fail to mention the play in research on Canadian drama, and not only because Voaden was an active contributor to the theatre. Studying in Germany, he was also attracted by the theories of Appia, Craig and the expressionists. Under Eugene O'Neill's influence, Voaden examined the possibilities of relocating European theatre theories and applying them to the landscape and milieu of north America in general, and Canada in particular.

Despite important differences in artistic motivation, cultural context and the type of social involvement, there is an amazing similarity between *Hill Land* and a number of early Hebrew plays written in Palestine that were also influenced by the combination of expressionism with notions of the Gesammtkunstwerk. Plays such as *Life*, by Badder, *Bonfires* by Carmon and certainly *This Land* by Ashman[17] are "basically a kind of ritual drama ascribing magical powers to the elements of earth and sky. The earth becomes a god, the pioneer victim becomes the victim of the earth, but the reconciliation with the earth will be in unity with the sky."[18]

In both the Canadian and Hebrew plays we find attempts to create "a new covenant" with a country, a culture and a new milieu through an active, theatrical interpretation enlisting the elements of earth, water, air and fire, with an extra emphasis on the earth. This is true both for the text of the play and the modes of its theatrical performance. *Hill Land* and *This Land* not only deal with pioneers as their subject matter, but they themselves are pioneering drama. In trying to describe the fusion of the main characters into a new physical space, the protagonists are presented in a process of mental and spiritual initiation, and indeed in a *quest* towards a remolding of their being according to the choice they have made to live in a new place, whether Canada or Israel. The new physical space is demanding, uncompromising and forces the dramatis personae to make existential rather than purely emotional choices.

Willpower, an indispensable dramatic element, is put to the test. The struggle with Canadian or Palestinian space is the main conflict of both plays, in contrast to realistic drama, and it is a struggle between two sorts of human (or divine) justice. In this sense, both plays are pathos-ridden and courageous attempts to challenge offstage with a specific theatrical expression of space as experienced in life, although only a small part of it can be presented on any theatrical stage. Both plays celebrate a victory over space, usually in terms of a reconciliation between the inner experienced space and the outer geographical one, as presented at the meeting point of the designed space of the set and the text on the stage. When the "celebration" is consummated the protagonists achieve social reconciliation. The land is no longer "mine" but "ours" is heard at the end of *Hill Land*, and the very same words are used in *This Land* (p. 24). There is an especial reconciliation, cathartic in character, of the hero with the victims, after he himself has gone through a *via dolorosa* of sorts. The religious significance of this dramatic move is not impaired despite the absence of any god, Christian or Jewish, since nature itself is elevated to a mystical level. In the Hebrew play, the historical aspect is united in an apotheosis with Man, where Nature is the path; in the Canadian, Nature unites with Man, and the hero is privileged to pass from mental insight to spiritual enlightenment.

Many biblical allusions are used in both plays, especially the Jewish myth of the preparation of Isaac for sacrifice, which, in

Christian eyes, was often seen as a prefiguration of the Crucifixion. ["Agnus Dei qui tollis peccata mundi."] Ashman also brings in analogies to Joel, the prophet of redemption, and Hannah, of the prophet Samuel's mother, who sacrifices her son to serve Eli the priest (as well as the story of Eli and his sacrilegious sons). In *Hill Land* Nora is the prophetess, the seer and the pioneer of a new life[19] and Paul's name and role evoke that of Christ's apostle. In both plays there is an altar and a sacrifice.

Both works employ the element of time in a mythical way, as well as the cycles of the seasons, the hours of day and night, the light of the moon, the sun and the stars; at the same time, they use fire as an image for the inner fire of the characters. One of the main axes of tension stretches between high and low, between the hill and the plain, between the banal and the sublime. Water is a purifying element of life, but also of death. Spring is not only a symbol of life, for resurrection is also death.[20] Parallel to cosmic time, human time is also well perceived in both plays. In *Hill Land* we are told "But we of the second generation are in between. We do not belong to either land." This is an indication of the playwright's awareness of the yearning for the land rather than the conquering of it, and of the tension between sky and earth, an image of the spirituality which will be achieved, if ever, only through striking roots deep into nature.

Both plays use a great deal of movement, for dance attaches people organically rather than in a rational way to their surroundings. It is through movement that people in fact shape their space, sculpt it and imprint their personal mark on it. Movement between sky and land makes a person a self-conscious adaptor between nature and the cosmic spirit, in both of which he or she is totally immersed. It is the poetry in *This Land* which carries the word of the pioneers upward to the sky; music does the same in *Hill Land*, a play rich with sound effects. In both the use of these primal modes of expression may be seen as an organic and holistic approach to nature and dramatic creation.

The external style of *This Land* seems much more realistic than that of *Hill Land* as regards to characters, structure and plot. There is a family, father, mother, son and a more distant relative, Hannah, who does not have children and who gets the final speech: "I do have grandchildren." She becomes the mythical mother of the tribe. Around this nuclear family live many settlers, workers and a physician. The real estate dealer is also described as a doctor; the one cures people and the other heals "the sick soils" of the swamp. The doctor is the *raisonneur* in the play, and it is he who draws the parallel between the pioneers and the plants. Like him, there are other characters who are not "round" but models of allegoric tendencies rather than people of flesh and blood. Voaden's decision concerning his characters is clearer. The nuclear family in *Hill Land*, Nora, Jane, Rachel, Paul and a doctor (here too) is surrounded by choral voices of personifications of human states of consciousness, as though the classical Greek chorus were divided into ten different roles given to individuals and small groups who maintain a deliberately metaphorical dramatic stand. The similarity between the Virtues and the Vices in this play and in medieval theatre is certainly not incidental (and perhaps the role of the Doctor is reminiscent of Chekhov).

Both plays try to shape an inner reality, each in its own way. Voaden's social and certainly political commitment is noticeably slighter than Ashman's. He does not seem to owe allegiance to anyone, and in this respect, his play is a rather lonely meteor in the dramatic skies of Canada. Ashman, on the other hand, enlists his theatrical talents – he was the most outstanding Hebrew playwright of the forties – to develop a myth "which will unite the people and endow them with a surge of deeds,"[21] meaning the Zionist pioneering spirit, especially in a period when the traditional religious Jewish background was deliberately laid aside and could not provide a lever for the pioneers. The renewed challenge of Jewish history in the land of Israel necessitated social effort, since a lone pioneer could obviously not achieve very much. Ashman was influenced not only by Soviet theatrical genres and German expressionism, but also by the need to remould a new ritual attitude for a group of people who had recently rejected a displaced culture, unrelated to the earth to which they had come and who were yearning to be accepted by the earth itself. Ashman also tried to reconstruct the people of Israel's former connection with their land, since uprooted entities required extra care when thrusting deeper into the same land two thousand years later.

In contrast to the "religion of work," in Gordon's ideas that influenced Ashman, Voaden developed a post-romantic nature religion, and, influenced by Wagner, depicted attempts to unite with the elements of Canadian nature. This, then, was the existential choice made by his characters. In his mise-en-scène the emphasis was on "antithesis between the old world and the new . . . "[22] Both plays lend themselves to Freudian and Jungian interpretations. Images of a tomb *qua* womb are frequently repeated, as are images of conquering the land compared to conquering a woman, as well as Sisyphian and Tantalic images.

In both cases the lighting is an important factor. Voaden, with more financial resources and a well-exploited modern stage, uses lighting as a spiritual element, emphasizing differences between light and shadow as well as manipulating colors to reveal harmony and melody, all of which could be achieved with the fine technical means at his disposal. Ashman, with fewer means, depicted entire seasonal cycles rather precisely; the different colors of the bay, the grey of dawn, a sombre winter, the dark of night, the light of noon, as well as different types of farms. The stage lighting, as a physical means of expression, no less than the set design, transfers both plays from one level of reality to a higher one, and dramatically and theatrically enhances their supernatural intentions.

In both plays the main struggle takes place between man and his still unfamiliar space; since he has come from the outside, he brings his consciousness to a consciousness-less space. On a deeper level the plays deal with making "neutral" space absorb human consciousness and spirit. With various degrees of success, and sometimes falling into the trap of oversimplification and a certain amount of melodramatic cliche (an inevitable result of the attempt to rise too high), both playwrights impose a sense of experienced space over the fictional stage space, imposing also a perception of mythical space on the real space of their surroundings.

It is not by chance that the visual perception of theatre in both cases was linked with groups working in the visual and plastic arts: the Canadian group of seven and, in parallel, the Beza'lel School of Art in Jerusalem, which revolted against the utopian idealism of the teachers of those years. Avi-Shaul, in his play *Among the Ruins* (1928), criticizes a painter who paints still life, arguing against his passivity. "I will paint living nature! land! living breathing earth." Voaden, with the same kind of understanding that dramatic modes of characterization are closely linked with painting, wrote an entire play about the painter Emily Carr.

Thirty-five years after *This Land* and some forty years after *Hill Land*, two more plays were written that take up an ironic stance towards the pathos of unity with the earth: John Murrell's *Further West* (1985)[23] in Canada and Yaakov Shabtai's *The Spotted Tiger* (1985)[24] in Israel. Where *Hill Land* had relinquished naturalistic modes of expression, and *This Land* had maintained realistic dramatic conventions, at least externally, both being in effect plays of myth and ritual, the two later works exploit a stylistic point of view based on a collage of scenes. In retrospect, a certain unity of message is achieved in criticizing the myth through actively using it and presenting a more ironically distanced point of view, addressed to the social and dramatic values in which the plays themselves participate.

Both these more modern plays are constructed around a central image that pulsates within them and interprets each scene and each character in its relation to the centre. The world, and Canada specifically, is described in *Farther West* as a brothel, and in *The Spotted Tiger* Israel is a circus, or at least in dire need of one. Both plays deliberately use historical materials and allusions to other plays. Shabtai draws on the pioneering myth of the twenties in Tel Aviv, on the ideology of anarchist Marxism, and on the disappointment of many of the pioneers with the faulty realization of their dreams. He also makes use of certain fantastic elements discernible in other plays of the seventies, and of an accepted tradition of absurd plays in which the hero's illusions are finally totally destroyed and he is shown at the end of the play emptied of everything he ever had, as in Ionesco's *The Chairs*.[25] In fact, the empty space itself becomes a metaphor for inner emptiness.

Murrell uses for his starting point a newspaper chronicle about a prostitute from Calgary and her lover, who shot and killed each other in a hotel room. His is a quest play, revealing station after station of the drive westward; until the protagonist reaches the Pacific ocean where he faces the challenge of himself and of his physical and social environment.

Both plays describe an important period of national consciousness; that of the twenties in Israel and the late eighties and early nineties in nineteenth-century Canada. The musical element is very important, with a pianist accompanying part of the section in *The Spotted Tiger*. In *Farther West*

> sounds are not part of a realistic background but a poetically arranged orchestration, complementing the words. (. . .) The meaning of Farther West cannot really be grasped without the study of its music (both words and music written by the playwright) and how it serves to contrast and support the text, expressing and underlying a world of yearning and innocence beneath a violent physical reality.[26]

It is not by chance that Shabtai and Murrell owe a debt to Chekhov, who also made extensive use of offstage music and voices. The above quotation could easily also describe the music of *The Spotted Tiger*, a music that does not succeed in veiling a harsher reality. Thus the music is a counterpoint to the visual aspects of the play. Both writers make careful use of lighting, like Ashman and Voaden, but in a more elegant and less strident way, in passing through the entire rainbow of the seasons and the hours, from cold morning light to glowing noon, with many suggestions for dusk and dawn which are particularly evocative. While Murrell often moves between interior and exterior locations, most of Shabtai's scenes occur in outdoor coffee houses, street restaurants and on the sidewalk. It should be noted that *The Spotted Tiger* takes place along the Tel Aviv beach area, on the borderline between land and the Mediterranean. Metaphorically, *The Spotted Tiger* begins where *Farther West* reaches its final border.

The protagonists of *The Spotted Tiger* expect redemption from the boredom caused by the combination of Tel Aviv heat and humidity, and mental desiccation. Noah says "seventeen years . . . " and Shoshana replies "We've waited so long." Pinek, the main character, is haunted by the mediocrity of the others. May Buchanan, the prostitute in *Farther West*, is driven by the puritanism of her environment, escaping not only from something but also to something: to herself as a liberated woman trying to shape her own fate in an oppressive society; one whose Eros is not only sex, but Eros in the broader sense of sensuality, joy of life, creativity and energy. Pinek too is the happy person, the crazy one, more grotesquely delineated than May Buchanan, grasping at balloons which will of course explode in his own face and in the face of all the other characters he is trying to sweep along in his glittering yet totally unrealistic royal circus. Both main characters in these plays are greater and more generous than all the other players. Both try to bring at least a certain redemptive solution to their worlds, whether through sex or through the circus. Both are located in a private space that may bring pleasure – illusory but perhaps more real than reality.

The endings of the two plays clearly testify that their continuation lies in other areas of reality. "On, on" it says in *Farther West*, and *The Spotted Tiger* ends with Pinek being killed in a duel of all things, an inevitable death caused by his own absurd yearnings. In a typical death rattle, he mutters "Ha, ha, mummy . . .

the world" and Max, bending over Pinek's corpse, says "Idiot!," as the cold light of dawn rises. May Buchanan also dies: "No more escape for you, my lady!," and also from a gun shot. Both are not only larger than their neighbours, but also than life itself, and thus they are doomed to die.

In *The Spotted Tiger* the value-oriented and political aspects are very clear. It is a play about the loss of the pioneering spirit, of failure, and of the need to find consolation on another level of reality. If this cannot be achieved, the seeker must leave to search for still another reality. Small towns in Canada must be fairly similar in their drabness to Tel Aviv of the twenties. From a universal, psychological, and existential point of view, there are probably few differences other than the climatic between Sheep River in the north-western territories, and a newish little town on the shores of the Mediterranean. In *Farther West*, the psychological description is more profound, but both plays, like their predecessors, and despite their more realistic façade, are still ritualistic. They begin in summer and end in winter; both traverse the seasons of the year as images of mental states and both are keenly conscious of the heroes' failure at self realization. The hope for a new king is presented as ironic in both cases.

Whereas the Canadian quest play takes place over thousands of miles of inner and outer hauntedness, the Israeli play finds refuge in voyages to the world of imagination, since the designed space in the work is in any case blocked by the Mediterranean and one cannot go any farther west in Israel. It is important to note that the purity, the freedom achieved, even though ironically, in *Farther West* with Seward's eulogy over May, is denied to Pinek who even at the end wants to be somewhere else: "Greece, Brazil, America. I will be very far."

The offstage of *The Spotted Tiger* is the world of disappointment and the "not here" of the characters. In *Farther West* offstage absorbs the quasi-realistic modulation of space in the quest westward. In fact, throughout the plays an experienced fictional space is shaped, a liminal threshold-like space; between sanity and insanity, internalization and exteriorization; precise poetic attempts to flirt with the *beyond* while increasingly aware of the hopelessness of the endeavour. In both these modern plays, unlike their counterparts of the previous generation, the inner space of the character has the upper hand; the more conscious space wins. In the contest between the inner space and the mythical space of *This Land* and *Hill Land*, both relinquish mythical space. One generation later, *This Land* by Ashman is re-examined and found insufficient, and *Hill Land* too calls for a renewed critique, sending May Buchanan from Voaden's lofty hill to the shores of her own ocean.

4

Oppressed Space

If we align the circles of dramatic space on and offstage, moving from the universal to the local, and to social and political space, we realize the similarity between human inner space, experienced as an image, and the actual architectural and geographical space which surrounds and also infiltrates individuals as well as groups of people. Gaston Bachelard's book *The Poetics of Space*, is devoted to the poetic connections between these two sorts of spaces; it is a phenomenological approach to "reading" houses and rooms, closets and drawers. But rather than the "topophilic" attitude,[1] implying a "happy space," as he calls it, we shall here examine spaces experienced as strange, unhappy and hostile. There is an important medium-oriented difference between modes of presenting space in literature and the concretizations of space required by actual theatre performances. Not always do the characteristics of real space overshadow the traits of the imaginary one,[2] to paraphrase Sartre's words on the sculptor Giacometti. Often, and especially in theatre, which is indeed closer to the three dimensionality of sculpture than to written literature, a genuine struggle exists between imaginary and real spaces.

In theatre such a struggle takes place within the souls of the living characters, as well as in the efforts of the actors to express the conflict in their stage behaviour and movements and in their relationships to the stage space around them. So far we have dealt with the attempt to make absentees present on stage through active use of the offstage void and by distinguishing between local and universal elements, as well as with certain aspects of the fertile clash between real and mythical spaces; this chapter will deal with dramatic characters who are considered strangers from a social and personal point of view as the protagonists of the play see them. They can be perceived as dwelling in a strange space, simultaneously remote, attractive and repellent, "dangerous," worthy of conquest, modification and adaptation. As such this kind of space is charged with dramatic tensions and conflicts, not necessarily solved, but always experienced as polarized and therefore very specific.

As part of the effort to actualize space in performed drama through sets, costumes and lighting, movement and voices, in addition of course to the acting itself, we shall examine how the feeling for the stranger's space is expressed in the perception of Indians and Inuit in Canadian, or Arabs and Bedouin in Hebrew drama. We shall also see whether these figures occupy a different dramatic space. The assumption is that inasmuch as "absence" can be "very present" and act as "negative presence"[3] so the space of such figures can be conceived as offstage.

In an article on the images of Australian Aborigines and natives of New Zealand and Canada in literature, Terry Goldie remarks on the prominent absence of the Aborigine in Australian literature, and talks also about the shift between writing from the outside and writing an inner identification, about "natives."[4] Margaret Atwood in the chapter titled "First People," in *Survival*, on Indians and Eskimos as symbols, clearly shows the images of the native inhabitants to be projections and wishful thoughts of the Canadian soul. On the one hand, the Indian is presented as inferior to the white man; on the other, he is idealized. In both cases he is doomed. In the description of Brebeuf's voyage she describes how a fortress is built to enclose the settlers and into which are allowed only those Indians who accept civilization and Christianity. Even when they submit to the culture of the conqueror, they are incarcerated in a prison within a prison.[5]

Often the process of physical and commercial colonialism was accompanied by cultural colonialism. The conqueror imposed on the conquered not only the power of the sword and the gun, along with alcohol and glass beads, but, and necessarily so, his concepts of religion and culture and his perception of humanity in general and space in particular. However, there is also the inevitable feedback from the conquered to the conqueror, affecting the same aspects. First, in the shape of non-obligatory and generally romantic notions, and later on as an infiltration of the deeper influence that the local spirit of the conquered imposes on the conqueror to a considerable degree.

Whether Canadian and Israeli playwrights present Indians and Arabs as well realized figures in their plays, or whether they inscribe them in contours of empty spaces, these figures of the strangers in our places, the alien within ourselves, those whose places we have taken, are quite conspicuous. This delineation of the empty contour can be compared to "carrying the void as a snail carries his shell."[6] Contrary to what Sartre may have meant, the stage void of the Indian and the Arab as strangers is filled with contents not so much aesthetic and existential as moral, social and political. To borrow another image from sculpture, one can compare the hollows of Henry Moore's works to the space some-times occupied by ethnic minorities in Canadian and Israeli drama. Margery Fee concludes her article on national romanticism with the words "marginal cultures can rarely afford to be cynical about nationalism: we are afraid that if we don't believe in Indians, we will have to become Americans" (America here means the United States).[7] Whether ignoring the character of the conquered minority and from a socio-artistic point of view this is a resounding evasion – or describing minorities as either much above or much below the level of the describer, the dialogue of equals is avoided, a dialogue that would necessarily influence drama.

Since the beginning of Jewish settlement in Palestine in the 1880s, many books, poems, plays and articles have been written on the subject of the Arabs who were already living in the country when the Jewish immigrants arrived. Few Hebrew writers and poets have not devoted at least some of their work to a description of the Arabs, their way of life of their contacts with Jews. Naturally, some of this writing was highly self-conscious in representing what was perceived as the encounter with an alien whom history had caused to be present at a time and place when circumstances were leading the Jews to return to their homeland.

The abrupt transition from the Diaspora to the promised land called for a deliberate effort on the part of the new immigrants to change their way of life to suit their pioneering ideology and high level of motivation. The ideology acted as a filter through which the experiences of the new land were absorbed, not always in their true colors. At all events, it is clear that the re-awakening occurred, as both cause and effect, at the height of a national identity crisis; each individual pioneer carried his or her burden of a complete break with the past and a hope of restoring body, spirit and soul in the present and the future. Zionism, then developing from a religious yearning into a national and social movement, was able to ignore the fact that the land was already partially settled by another people.[8] Hebrew writers, however, began to recognize "the other" in a literary form, a process that reflected the contradiction between national aspirations and individual encounters.

The proliferation of modern Hebrew literature on the Arabs does not, for the most part, deal with the Arabs as such, but is generally an attempt by the writers to reinforce *themselves*, and achieve some sort of national self-hood. The Arab in Hebrew literature often appears only as a fictional object or motif (with a realistic and concrete façade) by means of which the Hebrew author proposes to delve into his *own* identity.

During the early period, when there was little obvious dissension between Arabs and Jews, the dominant depiction of the Arab was in romantic and exotic terms. In the writings of Smilansky, Stavy, Reuveni, Hurgin and others, Arabs in their swirling robes ride their fiery steeds across the desert sands, with the east wind blowing against their black hair and noble sun-scorched faces. Traditions of blood-feuds, oppression of women, hospitality to strangers, and the like, held a magical attraction for the Hebrew writer who had recently left a small East European town. Of this group, some spoke Arabic and were directly inspired by the Arab milieu. Although set out to describe the everyday life of the poor *fellahin*, their work was dominated by what they saw as the magical spirit of the son of the desert, in the style of Byron who longed for the glories of ancient Greece, or nineteenth-century Americans who wrote about the Red Indians. These works idealized reality while imposing their own wishes and preconceptions on it.

The Arabs were perceived as a sort of continuation of biblical times – a period to which the first pioneers wished to return, to demonstrate that they too had roots in the Holy Land. The second President of Israel, Yitzhak Ben-Zvi, devoted much of his time to searching for the Bedouin tribes who, according to traditional sources, were the ten lost tribes of Israel. Rachel Yannai, his wife, relates: "My eyes were fixed on a Bedouin . . . he reminded me of our [Jewish] Yemenite brothers. Something close. Purebred . . . "[9] Many writers latched on to the old, easily identifiable Hebrew versions of the names of Arab villages, and in this way proposed to link themselves with their past through the Arab inhabitants. The attitude to the Arabs in early modern Hebrew literature was an attempt to understand the Arabs and Arab culture as a channel leading back into the past; an identity was sought, and created, for the Hebrew writer who had returned to his homeland.

The romanticization of Arabs and Arab life was a sort of literary refuge from a sometimes not too cheerful reality. Encounters with impoverished Arabs, pedlars, donkey drivers and *fellahin*, armed bandits and urban petty criminals, provided material for romantic/exotic descriptions, as long as the writer himself, or the group of people with whom he most immediately associated himself, remained unharmed. As the Jewish–Arab conflict escalated, romanticism disappeared, leaving its impressions to be used only as material for ironic or nostalgic attitudes in the hands of later writers such as Kenaz, Kenan and Levin. The "romantic" wave in Hebrew literature came to an end because of changing literary fashions and because reality rejected the connotations imported from eastern Europe. Nonetheless, at the base of this romantic conception – a naïve and soft-hearted one – can be found a line of thought typical of the entire approach to the Arabs: the "literary Arab" was a tool in the hands of the Jew in search of his own identity. It is hard to believe that Hebrew writers who dressed and behaved like Arabs and mingled with them, really wished to become Arabs, but it is a reasonable assumption that their approach was based on the desire to examine their supposed historical roots. Moreover, the Jewish pioneers had rejected a mainly religious and urban Jewish tradition in order to renew and rebuild themselves in the country of their forefathers, amidst its scenery, agriculture and land, and achieve, rather like the "Narodniki," a national, personal and spiritual renaissance through a mystic communion with the very soil of the land.

We must distinguish, therefore, between a historical nostalgia for the Jewish biblical past and the nostalgia linked to the writers' personal memories. When writers such as Nachum Gutman or Benjamin Tamuz recollect the years before the establishment of the State of Israel, such memories are linked to an image of a small, intimate country, – a non-industrialized, pioneering and optimistic Land of Israel. They are also bound up with the Arabs who populated the Sharon area, for example, and who maintained commercial dealings and relatively good relations with the Jews. Writers' descriptions were dominated by aesthetic elements – oriental arches, costumes, marketplaces, colors, scents, camels, and so on. These writers generally tended towards non-political writing; their nostalgia was often an effort to come to terms with current hostilities. The Arab, when perceived in this way, was often a close friend whom the troubled times had distanced from his Jewish companion. Sometimes the Arab was portrayed as a symbol of profound agricultural roots: the Jewish settler wished to inherit such deeprootedness together with the land that he had purchased.

There is also, of course, the approach that looks at the Arabs directly and not as objects (willing or unwilling, conscious or unconscious) within the concept of Jewish identity and linkage to the renewed land. This approach, not romantic, nostalgic, exotic, or otherwise complicated, simply describes the Arabs as family men, merchants, competitors, doctors, and the like. Realistic in style, for the inherent problems of religion and politics involved in depicting a different nationality were not ignored, this approach did not describe Arabs *despite* their being Arabs but, rather, because they were Arabs. No "humanistic" whitewashing was undertaken; rather, attempts were made to come to terms with the problem and the people. David Shachar (who lived in the mixed quarter of old Jerusalem) and Shulamit Har-Even wrote their plays on this basis.

In the seventies "probably the strongest impression made by Canadian plays . . . was the theatre of the underdog and the outsider." [10] The Jews, however, had lived in Israel before they went into exile and in this they differ from the Canadians who dispossessed the Indians without having an historical document of religious, cultural and geographical authority over the land. Certainly the contemporary validity of the old proprietorship is debatable between Arabs and Jews, who are still struggling over the twice promised land. Therefore the role of the Arab in Israeli theatre differs from that of the Indian in Canadian theatre; not to mention the fact that the vast area of Canada is not surrounded by some two hundred million Indians and 22 Indian states. In Canada, the Indians have long been virtually eliminated, whereas Israel faces a growing Palestinian minority within the country, the hostility and huge economic resources of the neighbouring Arab countries, and its own political short-sightedness. Thus, the role of the Arab in Hebrew drama differs from that of the Indian. First, the image of the Arab is a *conditionally* liberal one. The chances of the Indians returning to their past power are rather slim and literary generosity can be afforded by people who do not feel threatened. The struggle over land and space in Israel is far more material, though not necessarily more moral. Every particle of Israeli land is drenched with historically, archeologically and politically exclusivistic notions, whereas in Canada only some 10 percent of the land is privately owned and spoken for. Despite these differences, however, there are still a number of similarities between representations of Arabs in Hebrew drama and Indians in Canadian.

The Inuit, farther from the eye and from the heart, had a play written "about" them by Henry Beissel, a Canadian playwright of German origin, called *Inook and the Sun*. This is a typical example, not necessarily of attempts to mould a Canadian identity, but rather to use Inuit *rites de passage* as applicable to any adolescent anywhere. A parallel Israeli version might have used Bedouin initiation rites without saying a word about the real lives and troubles of that people.

Under the classical European influence of Shakespeare's Shylock and Lessing's Nathan the Wise, Israeli playwrights too were inclined in the earlier years to present either an enhanced or a diminished image of their Arab characters. On the right side of the political map there was fear of "dangerous" humanization of the Arab and on the left, a fear of dehumanization. This may partially explain both the relative absence of Arab figures and the non-realistic polarizations in their representation when they did appear in drama.[11] In the seventies the late but welcome change took place, as the Arabs slowly began to be liberated from their captivity in Israeli literature – namely, from functioning as a metaphor, an image and a symbol for the use of the self-searching Israeli – and started to assume flesh and blood, and equally, a spirit and a self of their own. In the *Governor of Jericho* (1975) by Joseph Mundi, although an Arab girl plays the symbolic role of a harlot, like Rahav in biblical Jericho, the playwright at least tries to describe her from her own point of view. In the *Palestinian Girl* by Sobol (1985), the Arab character receives a much fuller and less symbolic depiction. In this play, although the element of self-reference sometimes weakens the political clarity of the message, it also enables the production to be better received, even by its political opponents.

In the eighties an increasing number of playwrights tried, with varying degrees of artistic success but a great deal of political zest, to create "real" Arabs in their plays. At the Acre Festival of 1987, a festival of experimental theatre presenting the creative attempts of dozens of Israeli theatre people, five out of nine productions in the official Festival competition dealt with the Palestinians' struggle for independence and their objection to Israeli oppression. These plays dealt directly and critically with the actual social and moral situation in Israel. In *Yesh Batikh* (*There's a Watermelon*) a prominent figure was that of a mute Arab. *The Zionist Whore*, a sharp political adaptation of Sartre's *La Putain Respectueuse*, seemed to present the State of Israel as a prostitute. The show called *Kafr Sham'a*, given by the Palestinian theatre "Al-Hakawati," was disrupted by a group of right-wing hooligans. In general, the entire 1987 Acre event was described as "too political" and not sufficiently "artistic." Six weeks after the close of the festival, the Intifada broke out. Retrospectively it became clear that even minor inexperienced playwrights had seen what leading politicians preferred to ignore. In addition to the rather ephemeral Acre festival attempts to describe Arabs and their real problems in modern Israeli drama, one should not forget such well-known playwrights as Hanoch Levin, Amos Kenan, and others who have given more and more space in their work to a representation of the Arabs.

Among the better known Canadian plays dealing with minorities, we find works by Harden, such as *Esker Mike, The Great Wave of Civilization*; *Riel* by Coulter; and certainly *The Ecstasy of Rita Joe* by George Ryga. Sharon Pollock has Indians in her plays *Walsh* and *Komagata Maru*, and Ringwood wrote *Maya* and *Drum Song*. Obviously, minor parts have been given to Metis, Indians and Inuit in many other Canadian plays. In some cases Indians were assigned non-speaking roles, which often meant a stage presence that brought weakness and deprivation into the centre of power in the play. However, the overall impression left after reading several dozen plays is that the motif of oppressed minorities is not a leading one in Canadian drama.

Five years after *Indian*, George Ryga wrote a no less explicit play, *The Ecstasy of Rita Joe*, about an Indian girl who, like "Indian," is deprived of basic economic, social, sexual and psychological rights. Like a metamorphosis of a Woyzeck figure, Rita Joe, like Coulter's *Riel*, is presented in a series of events, or "visions," connected with her trial for murder. This indeed is a unifying dramatic element, but in fact it is Canadian society that is on trial and not Rita Joe. In contrast to the basic respect shown to Sitting Bull in *Walsh*, or some of the figures in *Drum Song*, Ryga's play exposes the Indian's despair and accuses the White Canadians. He does so without sentimentality, although his division between the good guys and the bad ones is somewhat too obvious. "It's a play that scourges Canadian society – or, if you like, the Canadian system – for the appalling crimes, both social and spiritual, that are committed against the Rita Joe's of this world."[12]

The specific set design for the play space leads the spectator up a ramp. "In front of the cyclorama there is a darker maze curtain to suggest gloom and confusion, and a cityscape." In his directions, Ryga asks for the stage to be squeezed into the auditorium. His indications for the setting try to do away with external theatricality, and create (as he says elsewhere)[13] an inner mythology. Most of the didactic work in this production takes place in the conquered space belonging, as is suggested, to the Indians, and performed by the actors carrying the text, together with the sets. Ryga's choice of space, together with that of the actors and director, appears an intelligent one, and implies a humane and moral attitude to the problem of minorities: the *personal* space is the crucial one, since the woods, the prairies, the entire landscape and nature have already been lost to the Indians in reality; and therefore, perhaps, also to the audience of this particular play. The city suggested in the background is that directly experienced space in which white Canadians and Indians, actors and audience alike, participate. The human and more psychological approach is also apparent through the use of the singer, an "alter ego" to Rita Joe, who sees her from the point of view of a white liberal unable to fully understand the complexity of the problems of the oppressed. Rita Joe's "visions" similarly expose anxieties *because* of the lack of detailed external design: "the circular ramp that comprises the set traces Rita's futile journey through the play." The abstract form is the main major image for space, a voyage without a solution. In this sense, the playwright's idea for a set design is indeed a precise visual image for the significance of the play. It is a medieval play of sorts, but it carries no message of redemption and no external lever will extract the heroine from her plight.

In the staged plot of the play, the court is a "white" area; it is therefore alienated and represents Rita Joe from an oppressive white Canadian point of view, despite its attempt to provide a neutral and fair trial. But it cannot be fair according to the Indian social standards with which she grew up. Therefore she finds herself in multiple exile: as an Indian "owner" of the land, she is in exile within her own country; in terms of her moral background, in exile in the court and in prison. She tries to defend her geographic and personal spaces, but she is helpless.

As a Canadian play performed in the centennial year (1967) *Rita Joe* not only exposed an important subject, but also the ability of Canadian theatre to deal with it. Ryga shows the short-sightedness of white people in their attempts to understand the problems of the

Indians. However, the play does not deal with the Indians only. The tragedy expresses the wider sociological aspect, and is successful in finding a balance between artistic quality, specific Canadianism, and the ability to radiate international and universal messages. It is interesting that Canadian theatre critics were not too clear about the play's uncompromising and quite explicit demand, for a *change* in the situation. Here and there they fell into the trap of sheer aesthetic criticism of theatre and drama per se, the exact opposite of what Ryga had intended to achieve.

The play *Walsh* by Sharon Pollock shows the Canadians in the bystander's position of delivering the Indian chief, Sitting Bull, to the Americans, who murdered him in retribution for the massacre of General Custer and his men. As the story is well known in North America, the play concentrates more on the moral implications, and less on the events themselves. Although the Canadians were allegedly less cruel than their southern neighbours in the process of oppressing and exterminating the Indians, Pollock draws attention to their responsibility: "It is not Sitting Bull's doom, we can recognize, though he was the obvious victim. It is Walsh's doom, and our share in it as Canadians."[14] The stage as it is described transports spectators over a bridge out to the prairies, to the teepees and the feathered head-dresses; it has no specificity apart from the ruggedness appropriate to the story. From an acoustic point of view, as an excellent offstage characterization which presentifies realistically, metaphorically and symbolically the space surrounding the stage, the music lays emphasis on a broad echo as a sign of a vast, empty country and a place of far distances; this atmosphere of huge expanses is reinforced by the appropriate lighting.

Here, too, the unique size of Canadian space is expressed in the void on the stage. Adele Freedman criticizes the production she saw for having most of the events "happening" in loud, wailing voices offstage, with not enough taking place onstage. She also attacks the dimensions of the Saskatchewan landscape designed on stage and the explanations given in the show for the Indian "disc."[15] Here, too the structure comprises disconnected scenes and only when seen together do they successfully present the story itself and the huge space in which it happens, even though it seems to be taking place in a garrison. The white officer, Walsh, has to serve both his masters and the decree of his conscience. Pollock does not make life easy for herself as an author, trying to create a figure who is indeed torn from within and yet finally makes a decision against the moral precept, as in the historical event on which the play is based. Israeli playwrights too have treated this matter of capture, a motif which effectively pinpoints the problem of identity and sheds a special light on the problem of space. Often the conquerer perceives himself as invading a space which is not his. When he captures the native, the indigenous person, he in fact internalizes his captive's natural space, making him an exile in his own country. Awareness of the enemy's, the stranger's or the conquered space, becomes a criterion for the identity of the conqueror as well. The motif of the prisoner imprisoned in his own space, which is at the same time the space usurped by the conqueror, provides a dramatic conflict which lends itself readily to the theatrical event.

An interesting motif that focuses on the identity problem is that of the "prisoner." Four Hebrew short stories were written between 1949 and 1959 dealing with Arab prisoners who fell into the hands of Israeli soldiers during the War of Independence and the Sinai campaign; all four stories are told in the first person, partly for the sake of credibility and partly, perhaps, because they are genuinely autobiographical.[16] In two of the stories the prisoner appears as the central motif; in the other two he is an important, but not central, character. In three of the stories the prisoners are killed in the end. Their deaths are described as humiliating – senseless from the point of view of human existence, like all death – and serving no political, social or practical military purpose. In the fourth story, when the prisoner is released, his captor is left with a sense of personal failure. The prisoner motif in these four tales – and in a fifth story by A. B. Yehoshua that uses a prisoner in a more metaphorical sense – shows the Arab as an object and a tool, and is primarily intended as a measuring-stick for the Israeli writers themselves.

Shaham's story *The Seven* was written in the winter of the War of Independence in 1948. Twenty-five years later he said in his preface to a theatrical adaptation of the story: "I could not find it in my heart to alter the naïveté of the twenty-three year old who wrote this story; the innocent faith in the solidarity of a brotherhood in arms, and the need for a warning that the mines that we lay for others – might yet explode under our own feet." The story revolves round a Palmach commando regiment trapped on a hilltop in the War of Independence. It becomes apparent that seven landmines are positioned on the hill in unknown locations "and the map is lost." The soldiers know that all seven of them will most probably be killed. After the first soldier is blown up by a mine, relations between the men deteriorate, for the death of one of them increases the chances of survival for the others. "We commanded our men to leave," says the officer, "No one obeyed us. Oh, if you had only seen with what longing they followed our foot-steps . . . "

The trapped commandos capture a young Arab villager and order him to run around the hill so as to explode a mine. He refuses, tries to escape, and is shot; then, says Shaham, "This stranger, enemy, I was sorry for him – for not being killed by one of the mines, thus saving one of us; it was as if his death was wasted. Pointless." The next day the remaining soldiers catch another Arab prisoner, an old man. "I didn't beat him up and didn't order him to run. I removed his shackles and treated him as if he was my uncle. The old man was full of emotion and I was hardly able to stop him from kissing my hand, kissing over and over . . . he kept coming back to me like a dog to its kennel. I greeted him with a smile and thanked him for his services. No one has ever cared for me in that way before. In the end, he walked further and further away, stumbling across the ridge until his feet finally found the mine."

The end of the tale reinforces the point made in Shaham's preface: the seventh mine remains to be discovered. Clearly, Shaham is making an analogy between the attitude towards the two prisoners and the symbolism of the mine. Using human beings as objects is the real mine that has been laid and is about to explode at any moment. In this story the relationship towards the old Arab is not a "nationalistic" one, but purely personal. The Arab, here, becomes a human mine-detector, a role he also plays in other works that express Israeli consciousness. He is not even considered an enemy but merely, as it were, as an estranged step in the process of the life and death struggle of a group of Israeli soldiers, and a literary means of rendering moral degeneration in times of emergency.

Shaham's description of the old Arab sharpens the consciousness of life and death, not only of the Israeli soldiers, but of an alien, an enemy who does not belong to the group of close knit commando fighters: the value of *their* lives and safety is taken for granted not only by the biased reader, but also by a particularly well developed tradition of mutual responsibility in the Palmach units. Obviously, Shaham chooses an unpopular path by bluntly making the soldier see the old Arab's life as "useless." Tamuz, on the other hand, in "The Swimming Contest," relates to Abdul Karim personally, as a character who is part of his own life, and something of himself is also destroyed. Abdul Karim, who possesses a personal history, is accidentally killed, and his death too is senseless from the narrator's point of view. Not only are Jewish–Arab relations depicted as unbearable, but something also dies in the Israeli – both as a person and as part of a nation: "Here, in this backyard, I myself, all of us, were the vanquished."

In S. Yizhar's tale, titled *The Prisoner*, the situation takes place mainly in the hero's mind, in a style reminiscent of Camus' story *The Guest*, itself based on a motif taken from the tale *Mateo Falcone* by Merimee. The Merimee story presents a system of moral values in the name of which clearly defined actions are dictated and carried out. In Camus' story the Arab is released in the end, as the narrator acts according to his conscience and is ready to take upon himself the responsibility for his actions. Yizhar's narrator, an Israeli soldier, has no single system of moral values to determine his actions. In *The Prisoner* two tentative value systems exist side by side; the hero is torn between the two and ends up by taking no action at all – a clearly Hamlet-like situation, perhaps expressing adolescent uneasiness more than an evasion of real risk-taking and adopting an unequivocal stand. Here too the end of the story is irresolute, open, hesitant. " . . . There is another sort of sadness, a grinding away sadness, the sadness of uncertainty, the uncertainty of a waiting woman, the uncertainty of a life sentence, a very private uncertainty, and a different, more general uncertainty, that the sun will set and it will remain among us, unfinished."[17]

The hero knows that from a humanitarian point of view he should release the prisoner. In this story, as in those of Shaham and Orpaz, it is clear that the prisoner does not present any security risk and that his release would not cause any harm. The writers deliberately handicap themselves in their efforts to describe cases of detention in which moral considerations take precedence over military ones. However, in Yizhar's story, there is also another system of reasoning: What will the guys say? What shall I do, an order? – "And you, you have to release him, even if the fellow himself laughs at you, even if he, or somebody else, sees it as helplessness; even if your friends mock you, even if they ask you to avoid releasing him; and even if they send you to the military prosecutor . . . " Yizhar describes the Arab's capture, his interrogation and his transfer to another camp where, perhaps, he will be killed. Descriptions of "atrocities" caused a great deal of anger in the Israel of 1948, the year of the war in which the story was published.

The importance of the story lies not in its description of the

Arab, but in its internalization of the subject of imprisonment. The true prisoners are not the Arabs, but the Israelis. Their prisoners imprison *them* by means of the guilt feelings that cause Israelis to agonize over difficult dilemmas: how to remain an idealist, a pioneering Zionist, a socialist, an honest and fair person, and at the same time conquer and imprison others.

These stories were an important step in recognizing the Arab opponent; a stage towards, and not only from the literary point of view, freedom from being imprisoned in one's various spiritual uncertainties. Only recognition of the self-consciousness of "the other" – a recognition whose personal and political ramifications are remarkably similar – will enable true personal freedom. Self-consciousness is inconceivable and so too, for our purpose, is complete identity, without recognition of the self-consciousness and the independent personal and national identity of others.

The most striking play to deal with the Israeli occupation of the West Bank, and what it means to be conqueror and conquered at one and the same time, was written in 1984. It has not yet been performed. Even the anticipated ban by the censor did not help to promote the production and despite a court order rescinding the ban the Haifa Theatre has not taken up its rights to the play. *Ephraim Returns to the Army* by Itzhak Laor[18] achieved a tumultuous reading at Tel Aviv University, in an attempt by a group of left-wing friends and supporters to circumvent the then existing ban.

The play deals with a military governor in the occupied West Bank, who, together with his ambition to carry out his oppressive military assignments efficiently, also tries to let it be known that he is pro-Palestinian, pro-resistance and pro-PLO. Ephraim, the schizoid, self-pitying, soft-hearted, "macho" protagonist cannot cope with the juxtaposition of his real function and his yearned-for one. The main conflict, following a series of smaller ones, between on and off-stage occurrences develops after a Palestinian youngster is shot dead during a demonstration while throwing stones at Israeli soldiers.

Unlike other political plays, *Ephraim Returns to the Army* does not address itself to an already convinced audience. Even in the satirical scenes the play avoids two-dimensional political slogans and formulas. The author is spared such oversimplification by his abundant use of self-directed irony, of the sort that neutralizes the sting of shallow criticism. Laor confidently steers a path among those who "weep and shoot" – Israeli idiom for "liberal" soldiers who, instead of refusing to serve in the captured territories, bemoan the need "to shoot" and yet do so.

The classical unities of time, place and plot are applied in a novel way in *Ephraim Returns to the Army*. For example, the dramatic convention of character as understood in a realistic and psychological play is revealed here in flashes of situations and relationships that are correct and authentic only for short periods, in a specific time, plot and space that may change from moment to moment. Similarly, the stage character itself is not "the same" character but an ego-less collection of social, circumstantial, political, sexual and psychological encounters. In this play it is clearly implied that only they who admit to the existence of self-awareness amongst their fellows, may themselves receive the right to say "I."

A strong deconstructive inclination, from a dramatic point of view, is harnessed to a moral attitude. Here Laor succeeds in the rare feat of harnessing two major theatrical references to a highly histrionic (though very economical) play. His self-referential elements are enlisted in a moral cause and his "other" referential elements – social, political and ideological – avoid the habitual traps of two-dimensionalism, typical of didactic theatre.

The character of Ephraim is invented and carries none of the obligations that are generally linked to a real character. The scenery, props, lighting, movement and, mainly, the world of voices that surround the stage, are displayed in a compressed process of disintegration. Instead of cohering, the play explodes; instead of dramatic action there is a series of splinter events – a controlled, lingering dissolution that symbolizes the "message" of the play and is at the same time an integral part of it. The stage is the attenuated edge of whatever is happening beyond it, representing as well as presenting in an absolutely committed way, the *real* evils that happen "out there."

Ephraim Returns to the Army deals with an "enlightened occupation," a linguistic monster, whose logical inability to exist does not preclude a certain existence notwithstanding. Against the background of this contradiction the representatives of this enlightened occupation crowd into the office of Ephraim, the military governor. The entire play takes place within a space described at the outset as simply a functional and focused area for events to occur. Gradually the space gains meaning and an imagistic impetus. Instead of a technical centre for scenery and props, the military governor's room becomes a bunker, a gaol, a TV screen: "(after a long silence)

Who told you that I don't want to leave the room? I leave the room whenever I want to. (Pause) Just because someone told you that I don't go out of the room you think that I don't go out of the room . . . " and so on, until it is quite clear what is being talked about. Ephraim, in a mock-*Hamlet* "to exit or not to exit" monologue, turns his office into a mock-Sartre *No Exit* situation of his own qualms of conscience. The play's space, which is in the protagonist's head and thus metaphorically off-stage, is the place of political, social, legal and economic wrong-doings, and the place for administrative acts inflicted by occupying armies, even "enlightened" ones.

Laor alludes to War of Independence plays of 1948 and to "In the Negev Wilderness" and "Dudu," two sentimental heroic songs about war heroes. The allusiveness works in two directions and exposes both the source alluded to and the alluding target, particularly as the playwright is saying "There is no such thing. Soldiers in reality do not quote soldiers from plays of the past." Like Hanoch Levin in *Shits*, Laor also uses former literary responses as material for his bitter juxtaposition of bygone idealism with the present oppression of the Palestinians. A small poison dart is thus dispatched in the direction of Amos Oz, the liberal left-wing author of the novel *Another Place*, claiming that there *is* no other place (or country?), only the governor's room and only *it* may be shown on the stage, and only through it can be disclosed what is inside the chambers of the heart of the governor.

The story *Ephraim Returns to Alfalfa*, by S. Yizhar, provides an additional allusion: this Ephraim attempts a neat little rebellion against the collective values of the kibbutz, but in the end he decides to return rather than leave, accepting his friends' ideological conformity. Laor not only slaughters some holy quasi-mythological cows of the liberal Israeli left-wing – his potential supporters in moral and political issues concerning the occupation. He charges the very ideological fortress of the kibbutz movement by claiming, implicitly, that their spokespersons, like Oz and Yizhar, preach much better than they practice. By "misalluding" to common Israeli values, Laor succeeds in shifting well established points of view, catching his audience off-guard. They may even refresh their modes of comparing the past against this undesirable present.

With deliberate intention, Laor eliminates any remnants of realistic illusion. He reveals the fictionality of his text and puts it to a test of psychological hygiene. The effort demanded from the reader/spectator is far greater than that demanded by an exclusive emotional commitment to the fiction of theatre.

Following and paying explicit tribute to Brecht, Ephraim and his lieutenant, Gedalia, are complementary contrasts like Puntilla and Matti, Shen-Te and Shui-Ta; so too are the characters of the young soldiers, David and Solomon. Their names, those of Hebrew kings, were not chosen by chance. The contrasting couples signify the soft versus the hard, left and right, mistress and wife. The play presents the soldier David as left-wing, soft-hearted and weak-willed; he wants to go and see the rock music group "Measures Taken" (deliberately named after Brecht's play). Solomon, on the other hand, is a Jewish fascist, firm in his convictions and capable of action; he kills an Arab demonstrator. David is actually in favour of the Arabs and shouts this semi-convincing message from the window of the room. Of the pair of women, Nehama, Ephraim's mistress, "consoles" (*nehama* in Hebrew) him sexually, while his wife Dvorka is deliberately ignored: "Be my big sister," he says to her. Ephraim, conqueror and conquered, experiences violent and impotent moments of love and sex in both the emotional and mental realms. Politics are stretched on the same axis. Ephraim changes character, language and style, ideas and affiliations during his stage existence, all according to his interlocutor and the immediate situation. The two-dimensional characters surrounding Ephraim are, in fact, only extensions of various states of consciousness of the protagonist himself and of Laor, his author.

Laor is not the only writer who depicts the Palestinian problem in his works. From *The Governor of Jericho* by Mundi to *Hamdu and Son* by Buton, through Grossman's *Yellow Time* and Habibi's *The Opsimist* (both have been performed in stage version), the question of occupation has been raised and debated in Israeli literature and the image of the Arab has developed from a two-dimensional caricature to a fully three-dimensional figure. The "literary Arab" – as an image in modern Hebrew poetry, prose and drama – was often a projection of the suffering conscience of the writer, perhaps even a literary captive. Here too, in depicting the Palestinian prisoner, Laor appears to be painfully aware of the cultural colonialism manifest in some of the work of his predecessors. He himself is not dealing with the conquered Arabs but with the subjection of the Israeli conqueror. His Arab character, the Palestinian prisoner, does not speak. The figure contains a condensed collection of the silences of many Arabs on many

Israeli stages, where some of these silences are deliberate and ironi- cal while others are simply a refusal to let the Arabs talk. Silent characters contain the compressed energy of the dumb, a slowly burning fuse.

The verbal violence Laor bestows on all the speaking roles does not stem from a sheer need for destruction. It is an attempt to make inroads into the dozing complacency of the occupiers. With the sad understanding that the theatre has no real power to uproot evil, Laor shakes up his dramatic characters on the stage in the hope that at least some small agitation will occur in the reader/spectator. Moral distortion exists not only in the occupation itself, but also in the selective ways and false satisfaction in which it is displayed. Real violence does not take place on the stage, as is well known, and the verbal vulgarities often used by the theatre, such as "sucking," "maniac" (Israeli for homosexual), "prick" have sent far fewer men to their death than respectable words like "Forward!" or "Follow me!."

Laor deliberately sets oversimplified, detailed realism, explicit and naïve, against stream-of-consciousness monologues, meticu- lously long, multi-layered and complex. A dramatic effect is thus created that does not permit pre-conceived reactions. This is not a "positive" play presenting alternatives. It makes a clear and definitive statement on the situation, saying "No!."

The play ends with a speechless scene: " . . . She gets up. Sits near the prisoner and again plays with a key she had hidden as the officer Gedalia came in. She plays with the key. The light slowly fades as she and the prisoner sit opposite one another. He is in handcuffs. She with the key. Dark."

The socio-artistic consequences of the Acre festivals and of a few off-fringe productions can, unfortunately, be summarized as well tamed experimentalism. With very rare exceptions, such as *Ephraim Returns to the Army*, Israeli theatre, repertoire and fringe alike, is on guard against the "avant garde" – especially if the latter is looking for political change. In a strange way, Israel does not need the theatre in order to be awakened.

Indian, by the Canadian George Ryga,[19] is a shorter and less sophisticated play than *Ephraim*, but no less effective in content; perhaps because of another sort of dramatic straightforwardness. First, space in *Indian* is completely open. The stage is supposed to be flat and grey with diametrical lines signifying a vast empty space. The fence is the main scenographic image of the play and it is soon made clear why it is the Indian himself who drives the poles into the ground, an act which seems *a priori* absurd and *a posteriori* stupid.

Like the Palestinian in *Ephraim Goes back to the Army*, the Indian is deliberately not given a first name. Lack of name in drama indicates the unattainability of a person's inner space. From other points of view, perhaps more religious or esoteric, one's name is the essence of being, as we know, for instance, from Jewish tradition, and from the modes of giving names in the Bible. Unlike the Palestinian, however, Indian does indeed open his mouth and speak, and does so very well. Laor, probably not wanting to serve as spokesman for the conquered, in order not to impose cultural colonialism on his dramatic "victim," makes his Palestinian into a silent character, an acoustic means of delineating an empty space. Ryga, on the other hand, lets his Indian direct the entire play and switch intelligently and with much sensitivity between various levels of linguistic expression, seemingly based on a simple vocabulary and a "distorted" syntax; at least in terms of correct prescriptive English. It is Indian's simple and strange language which emphasizes the gap between his poverty and his natural intelligence and potential for maneuvering, and especially the way in which he has learned and internalized the verbal and physical violence of his oppressors. "Ryga's Indian is not passive, dull or feeble; on the contrary, he is master of physical intimidation and psychological terror, subtle insults and brilliance of maneuvering rising from the desperation of a man who has nothing to lose . . . "[20]

Laurence Russell accuses Ryga of overly romanticizing the Indian character, because he wished to make him a more acceptable person, thus resorting to the paternalistic fallacy of the noble savage. This is exactly why Laor makes his Palestinian quite mute, endowing him with the violence of silence. Russell also claims that "Ryga has scored the essential mystical truth concerning not only the Canadian Indian, but man himself."[21]

The Canadian landscape of *Indian* is an open organic setting but also a hostile one, in which both the Indian and the white people are intruders who break up the flat, hot, grey harmony of nature, as the play describes it. The concluding scene shows Indian continuing to work; the closed besieged space at the end of *Ephraim Returns to the Army* has Nehama playing with the keys, debating whether to release or keep the prisoner. Both are a discussion of whether to release or keep the prisoner; both are dramatically harsh, no-solution endings. Through the use of imaginary inner space, designed as very open or very closed, Laor and Ryga demand a solution on the human and the political level. Despite a Marxist façade and a Brechtian dramatic syntax, both playwrights rely on a profound need of mythological elements, not only as allusions. Thus their plays avoid a two-dimensional, local agit-prop semblance. Human strength and universal arises ensue from a fair judgement not only of the oppressor but also of the oppressed. Ryga shows how his Indian becomes gradually more violent; Laor shows how his conquerers are partly, at least, soft and hesitant people. The credibility of the plays arises, among other things, from a deliberate blurring of the Indian problem, all the way to the horizon of the Indian problem, and of the pressure felt in a small, closed space of the Palestinian problem. In fact, the spatial image in itself is described as a stumbling block on the way to a realistic solution, since the space perception of the oppressed and the oppressor are necessarily and essentially different.

While *Boesman and Lena* by Athol Fugard deals with black, white and colored relationships in South Africa, through an improvised chat out of doors in this way rather resembling *One for the Road*, by the English writer, Harold Pinter, a tough investigation takes place inside. The very politicized plays by the South American Enrique Buonaventura happen somewhere between the outside and the inside; while *Catastrophe*, by Samuel Beckett, a play dedicated to the present president of Czechoslovakia, a playwright himself, takes place on the stage, as a stage, in a theatre. All these play-wrights in using either a closed or an open space in depicting an unclear offstage or in evoking fictional space by presenting it as a self-conscious theatre stage, want to harness the theatre in order to make truthful and painful statements about oppression. The closer the "stranger in his own country" is to his oppressors, so too does his space become more restricted. Finally, the conqueror himself finds himself conquered. External alienation has been internalized.

5

Presentations of Social Space

This chapter deals with the socio-artistic meaning of dramatic spaces in Canadian and Israeli plays, distinguishing between social and personal spaces in four particular plays, two from each country. *Balconville* (1979)[1] is generally considered the most successful work of a well-known Quebecois writer, David Fennario, who delivers a clear message, legible even beyond the borders of Canada. This is the first bilingual Canadian play in which the verbal gimick of using the two languages simultaneously on stage serves its purpose truthfully, humorously and sharply. It is a good representative of plays which permit Canadians living on the fringe of society to express the voice of "the other" Canada. Fennario, Marxist by conviction and no less so in his playwriting, has become the favorite of the media. What happened to the German playwright Franz Xavier Kroetz, to the Austrians Handke and Bauer and to many others, has also happened to Fennario: he has achieved commercial and artistic success as a result of the immense social fury he has vented against the society which now praises him.

A somewhat similar reception has overtaken Hanoch Levin, the author of *The Suitcase Packers*.[2] Hanoch Levin had started to write satirical political cabaret material comprising songs and critically barbed skits directed against the Israel repression of the Palestinians living inside Israel, and Israeli *hubris* generally, before the Six Day War in 1967. Later he wrote his own adaptations of classical plays and motifs such as *The Sorrows of Job* and *Everyman*, in which he examined the degree of Israeli sensitivity to the agony of humanity in general. *The Suitcase Packers* is one of Levin's "social and family plays," a category that includes most of his work so far, and which forms the focus of our interest in this comparison with Fennario's *Balconville*, a Canadian "neighbourhood" play.

On the theatrical stage a balcony is a metaphor for an external space, connecting the inside of a house with the street, other houses, etc. The inside of the house traditionally expresses the intimate psychological space, and the outside of the street the public and social area. The title *Balconville* is taken from the answer given by a poor Montreal citizen to the question where he would spend his summer vacation – in "Balconville." Here this particular "outside" is ironically meant as a holiday play for the poor. The balconies of the Paquette, Williams and Regan families are the focus of the plot. The set design represents "the back of a tenement in the Pointe Saint-Charles district of Montreal. We see a flight of stairs leading up to two balconies side by side, the Regans' and the Paquettes'. Directly below the Paquettes' balcony is the ground floor balcony of the Williams'.[3]

Four scenes in the first act and three in the second take place within close range of the balconies: in the lane and the adjacent street. But the visual focus of the events is mainly the balconies themselves. This housing project inhabited by French and English Canadians in the year of 1979, in which no one has a real chance, concentrates on the hopeless milieu of nine characters in a politically torn city, under the rule of the Partie Quebecois. As in the plays of Alan Ayckbourn and Dario Fo, which combine social criticism with comic elements, these nine characters will not be able to move away. (Fennario later wrote a play called *Moving* in which he re-examined whether and how social structures and mental modes can be changed by people who are perhaps not sufficiently deprived and not yet motivated to make things move; for the time being they still have too much to lose: beer and television programs.)

Hanoch Levin's seventeenth play, *The Suitcase Packers*, contains more than twenty-five characters who live in the same neighborhood and much too close to each other. The subtitle is "A Comedy with Eight Funerals." Close neighborhood existence is very well known to Israelis, very few of whom live in one or even two family homes. After the large-scale immigration to the State of Israel from 1948 on, many cheap housing projects were rapidly erected, and most of them are still inhabited. Lack of privacy, constant inter-penetration of sounds and smells, social tensions related to ethnicity and economic situation, each family's constant, intimate and intense involvement in the life of its neighbours – Israelis can easily identify the Quebecois tensions through their own filters. The collection of families and individuals in *The Suitcase Packers* live on balconies overlooking the street, and they are deeply implicated in each other's lives. They too are unemployed and watch the pseudo intimate cultural garbage generously offered by their television sets. They flirt, they gossip, they complain about inflation and the telephone service.

Whereas the house is the stronghold of the well-made realistic play, whether Ibsen's bourgeois house or Osborne's working-class tenement, the street is often an arena for plays of a more socially-oriented message such as Hauptman's *Weavers* and many of Brecht's plays. The balcony, as an image of a frontier line between the "inside" and the "outdoors," expresses the tension between the psychological and the social. The balcony itself can be perceived as a mask which the inside wears in its relationship to the street outside, at the same time filtering whatever comes from the street back inside.

When Genet was highly dissatisfied with the London production of *The Balcony* (1956), he remarked: "My play, *The Balcony*, takes place in a brothel, but the characters are as little rooted in the reality of whorehouses as those of Hamlet are rooted in the world of courts and courtiers."[4] Critics such as Lucien Goldman and Philip Thody saw the political and social messages of the play but only a few paid attention to the close relationship between the set design image and the meaning of the play according to the theatre's own criteria. *The Balcony*, as a significant name, as well as an important location in the play, is both a divider and a bridge between the outside and the inside. Genet here creates encounters between people who usually do not come together, and their meeting place emphasizes the profound discrepancy between the personally and socially desired image and the real essence, the weakness, the wickedness and the "perversions" of these same people. It is a play about human "balconism."

With Fennario, the message is less complex, and the vision more political. The Montreal balcony dwellers could be expected to rebel against their exploiting landlords, since the hostility between French and English in Quebec is, according to Fennario, nothing but a capitalistic class manipulation. The suppressed of both ethnic groups do not rebel since they are not sufficiently conscious of their situation. Their consciousness and their lives are not yet compatible. The play's message, together with the exploiting landlords and politicians, hovers somewhere above the poverty-ridden neighbourhood of Pointe St. Charles; physically and metaphorically it dwells on

Westmount Hill, the affluent "offstage" neighbor of the lives and actions of the poor.

Most of Levin's characters, on the other hand, are well aware of their impotence. As expressed by their obsessive packing of suitcases, all the characters want to get away, be somewhere else, in Rome, America, Vienna, Switzerland or London: "Not that I have any illusions concerning London. London doesn't wait for me. There, too, I will be alone. And perhaps that's already for life. to be alone. But in London there are more movies, better music, excellent television, people are much nicer, so that despair becomes more comfortable. Get it? If I must end my life like a bitch, let television at least be good television. Bye bye."[5]

Levin never explains what exactly that "other" place is; or for that matter, what *this* place is. But the audience always knows quite well where it is: in some Israeli ennui-ridden town. The departures from *this* place cannot be made to London or New York, only to the cemetery, with a short halt on the way in hospitals and old-age institutions. One rare scene occurs in a nightclub, depicting a night out, retrospectively understood as rather awkward, since it tears the audience out of the "natural" balcony ambience. Another episode is a conversation near a bus stop – because all the characters want to get out. Most of the scenes, however, take place realistically as well as metaphorically in the stage's everyman's land of the balcony. Night club entertainment and bus stop symbols of movement are mere illusions. Therefore, when Bella says "So far, mommy, don't accompany me any further" she uses one of the Hebrew sub-textual meanings of the word accompany ("le'lavot") – funeral ("levaya"). She wants to go unescorted to a "somewhere else," a place which is not a cemetery.

The two sorts of offstage[6] both in *Balconville* and *The Suitcase Packers* can be described as two concentric circles around the stage which wrap around each other and yet retain the limitations of the geometrical metaphor. Fennario almost ignores death as an encompassing entity, but emphasizes the surrounding social atmosphere. To Levin, nothingness is the dominant offstage element. He outlines the social offstage realm but refers mostly to the "big void."

Slightly more realistically, Tom, the youngster from *Balconville*, like Bella in *The Suitcase Packers*, also tries to reach New York, "another" place, but he too is let down by his too great hopefulness, which is perhaps more specific than Bella's but quite irresponsible:

"I dunno . . . it's a big place. Ya never know. I might find a job as a musician, ya know? Once I learn about, uh, major chords, minor chords. Shit like that . . . "[7]

He returns to his balcony on a very minor chord because he was not allowed entry into the United States. Levin's New York is an imaginary wishful thought, while for Fennario it is a particular city and particular conditions do not permit the character to reach it. Moscow, for Chekhov's *Three Sisters*, lies somewhere between the ideal, unachievable New York of Levin, and the realistic New York of Fennario. The economic or existential distance proves the impediment; not the physical one. Fennario presents Tom's attempts to extract himself from his situation as a typical Catch 22: Tom wants to get out in order to make money, but cannot do so since he has no money.

The first scene in Levin's play, which is characteristic of his writing as a whole, opens with Shabtai Shuster's heroic attempt to defecate after four days of constipation. Three days later he will die; metaphorically, because he couldn't get rid of his own shit. In fact, he suffocates in it. Fennario, more realistic, less desperate, and not as tough, uses a subtler image: Muriel needs an ulcer operation. The metaphor is clear. She too internalizes that which cannot be solved by political activity and struggle and she is psychosomatically subdued by her negative energies turned inwards. In both cases, the inner space of the characters is marked as poisoned. There are those who do not agree that illness is a metaphor,[8] but in theatre such images are necessary and very natural.

In yet another (deliberate?) variation on Chekhov's *Three Sisters*, *The Suitcase Packers* opens with "Sick father goes to the toilet. For four days he hasn't defecated. Maybe he will now," which is a deliberate shattering of Olga's pathos: "It's just a year since Father died . . . on your name-day, Irina." In *Balconville* a fire breaks out towards the end of the play, a direct threat by offstage to reality, as in *The Three Sisters*: "And when my girls were standing by the door in just their underclothes, and the street was red from the fire, there was a dreadful noise, and I thought that something of the sort used to happen many years ago . . . and at the same time what a difference there really is between the present and the past! And when a little more time has gone by . . . people will look at our present life with just the same fear, and the same contempt, and the whole past will seem clumsy and dull, and very uncomfortable, and strange." To Vershinin, who says these words, Fedotik replies laughingly: "The guitar's burnt, the photographs are burnt, and all my correspondence" (Act 3). In Fennario's play the tenants of the Pointe St. Charles building save their beer and their television-sets first; only once their dearest are safe, do they rescue the sofa as well. In order to extract the sofa, a number of people must work together to carry it out. At this point in the play, each spectator is invited to decide what he or she would save from a real or imaginary fire about to consume their own home.

The downfall of Fennario's characters lies in their attempts to conserve the illusory drugs of their lives, the physical and mental temptations. Vershinin's speech is echoed in Motke's lines in the last scene of *The Suitcase Packers*: "And yet, the one true thing we have to say we do not say . . . and soon, the earth will cover us too, when we lie here everything suddenly becomes very clear. What was important and what was trite, we know we had something else to say and we didn't say. We wasted our time, we chewed, we spat and didn't say . . . "[9]

Fennario's ending is political, ironic and much less existential: "Citizens of Pointe Saint-Charles, we live in a time when we need a strong government . . . Remember, a vote for Gaetan Bolduc is a vote for security, for justice, for law and order . . . and for the future. Le futur . . . "[10]

Instead of Fedotik's laughter in *The Three Sisters*, a Levin character remarks in response to "the one true thing we have to say," "it is so moving . . . so true . . . ," a double irony in which one character reacts with pathos to the nonsense uttered by the first. The real scorn is the playwright's. Fennario brings his characters together in a final tableau: "What are we going to do? . . . Qu'est-ce qu'on va faire?" And each group, the English and the French, asks the same question in two languages. Levin's last words are given to Elkhanan who, also in a quasi-group situation, says: "I will come soon"; actually promising that he will forever be on his way, never reaching anything anywhere. He becomes the suitcase of himself, the balcony of himself, neither inside nor outside, no longer here, not yet there. For existential reasons in Levin's case and direct political reasons in Fennario's, all the characters are essences of "almost," floating between the "no longer" and the "not yet." While Levin's conclusion is merciless in its pseudo-hopefulness, Fennario's is a question, perhaps a beginning of true action, and presented without irony. The space in both endings appeals to an open, indefinite outside.

Fire gives heat and light, but it also burns and consumes. It is a symbol for life and death, a polarized ambivalence of hope and despair, destruction and resurrection. Chekhov and Fennario let the light and heat of offstage fires reach the characters on stage, demanding that they make some kind of a decision. Since these characters have weak wills and are barely able to decide and act, the playwright sends them omens of warning and crisis as dramatic challenges and catalysts for taking on stage action, despite their inner emptiness. In this way, perhaps, the characters will be committed towards the outside reality and act rather than measure out their lives with coffee spoons.

Levin avoids fire and instead plants eight funerals in the play as existential warnings. His characters have long given up fire and its value-added symbolism, be it heat or destruction; but death, even of "the other person," as a reminder of one's own eventual finality, still makes them tick, weakly. The neighbourhood funeral becomes an entertaining ritual, a relatively intense pastime, as a way of living, and a proper substitute for fire. In scene seventeen the announcement of Abner's suicide is received like the alarm "fire" in Balconville. The uniquely local despair of Levin's very Israeli characters is expressed in their language and their wish not to be here, as their main motivation. These two aspects are modifications of a passive–negative attitude, a reaction to offstage demands. In this way, too, the characters' space is defined as a collection of feedbacks radiated to them from London, Vienna or an imaginary New York. Like sonar or radar, when the beam returns to its source, the space of the self is identifiable only in relation to the other. It has no authenticity of its own.

From a wider point of view, the inhabitants of Levin's small Israeli neighbourhood are a cross-section of the urban lower middle class. They go on their way with their petty desires to their even pettier sins. Their conflicts are dull and great human yearnings collapse into the basic needs of sex, defecation, food and comfort . . . and, no doubt, a trip abroad. Like the tenants of *Balconville*, "The Suitcase Packers" are forever stuck in passive readiness, lacking the ability to realize their wishes. The eight dead in the play are provided with an official local mourner, who will be mourned himself: "Dear so and so, today we take leave of you . . . " Levin's real and actual offstage is the grave, sometimes concretized onstage in little death-spaces of stretchers, coffins, and death beds.

The Suitcase Packers can indeed be seen as a play Fennario might have written if he had completely despaired of salvation for his characters through political action. In their despair, Levin's people are anonymous; they are only types, self-made two-dimensional characters, rather than real people; cardboard masks moving in empty space which designates the emptiness within them. They have no biography, only an accumulation of missed chances. Fennario and Levin both use the first-person plural at the end of their plays, like Chekhov. This, of course, embraces not only the characters on stage, but also the auditorium and the world beyond it. While Levin borrows from Chekhov the anxiety of existence, Fennario interprets the Russian playwright socially, as though the October Revolution is already lurking beyond the *Cherry Orchard*.

The set design for *The Suitcase Packers* was a huge empty black space with a dimly-lit narrow strip, on which the characters moved, mostly from right to left. The depth dimension of the stage was rarely used, and only in order to evoke some of the dead whom we, as audience, had already met before as living people and who now rejoined the story line. The actors employed a deliberately flat and manneristic style, intensifying the spectators' obligation to identify and fill in the emotional gaps. As human dolls, moving on a target board, the characters appeared mechanically motivated, devoid of independence, of thought, of feeling and will, except for their obsession with sex and entertainment. The text is bereft of sub-text but it is well provided with social and theatrical context. Since the characters have no depth, they are given deliberately flat language, like a sock which can be worn on either side. The suitcase, like the television-set in *Balconville*, is the main stage property, signifying the desire to "get away from here," an image of the people themselves: empty boxes with handles containing some unimportant objects.

Fennario and Levin's figures could be asked whether they would be willing to relive their lives, to be given the chance to live any part of their life again without being aware of this as an additional period; would they be willing to do so?[11] They might say yes, because life itself has a value, and therefore, a reconstruction of any part of it is a good idea. Or else, they could say no, life is difficult, superficial, haphazard and basically bad, and going through it once is quite enough. Levin's characters would give a totally negative answer, whereas the slim chance for improvement hovering over Fennario's people might generate a positive answer even though a more illusory one.

In a "neighbourhood" work such as *Our Town* by Thornton

Wilder, of *Spoon River Anthology* by Edgar Lee Masters, at least a minimum amount of charity can be found, ensuing from the playwright's sense of optimism, as well as from the hope of selling a happy end to a potentially interested audience. Also, human pettiness can be elevated to a poetic level as in Dylan Thomas' *Under Milkwood* or be satisfied with Chekhov's or Gorki's pessimistic irony which is nonetheless warm and sympathetic. Fennario certainly likes his characters, and together with them, he pities their hopelessness: " . . . Being poor is just more miserable and more boring than being rich."[12]

Levin is much more cruel to his figures, positing the chance for a solution only on the metaphysical level. The main protagonist here is Death, who dwells offstage. The solution for Fennario's character is to be found in Notre-Dame de Grace, cote St. Luc and Westmount, the richer neighbourhoods of Montreal, and in a more just division of capital, because "Being conditions consciousness." In Levin's approach the opposite is true. *The Suitcase Packers* is not a political play. Rather, it uses certain social materials and harnesses them to existential, human purposes. "The playwright shrugs his shoulders when he shows us the film on which this funny and sad procession is depicted, finally sinking into the darkness which foretells the darkness and blankness of our own end. Death is the hero and the real subject of Levin, behind his thousand masks."[13]

In an interview, Fennario was asked whether his characters are trapped because they can do nothing about the approaching fire: "Well, maybe not about their house but something has already happened. They have been forced to work together and to organize to keep themselves in that situation. That is a start . . . "[14]

Balconville, although some critics praised its dramatic qualities, is an explicitly political play: "The final scene in which the characters turn to the audience and ask: 'What are we going to do?' is straight out of the most bareface agit-prop skit."[15] Martin Knelman argues similarly: " . . . Fennario is far less impressive as a political thinker than he is a dramatist."[16] The play opens with the sound of a screeching car, and with Diane's refusal to go out, following a call from a boy offstage. Having a good time is a notion outside our space:

Paquette: Qu'est-ce que t'etais hier soir?
Diane: Dehors.

Paquette: Ou ca dehors?
Diane: Dehors, J'at'ai dit dehors.
Paquette: Dehors aved Jean-Guy . . . [17]

The five repetitions of "dehors" are not incidental. Later, interesting connections are made between theatrical space and the message of the play through the use of means of transportation. Thibauld's bicycle tyre is punctured. The steps in the house are broken, and people stumble climbing them. Paquette's car is out of order, and he tries to fix it violently, judging by the sounds offstage. Demolishing the car expresses Paquette's frustration, as he shatters his chances of getting away and moving on with his own hand. Thibauld is looking for an illusory vehicle in the image of a Honda 750 cc motorcycle instead of a bicycle.

The characters are sometimes presented in slapstick style, as a kind of interaction between neighbors who pour bread crumbs, spaghetti and water meant for boiling potatoes over each other's heads. The bad eggs aimed at the politician, Bolduc, hit the neighbor, Paquette. In oppressive regimes or even in a society which feels deprived, the oppressed or deprived are the first to be divided amongst themselves and the first to torment each other. Most of the telephonic communication with the outside in *Balconville* has ominous negative undertones. Only cultural junk food enters through the television set, distracting attention from the need to act socially, ideologically and politically. Tom sends a letter to his girlfriend on his way to New York, but since he cannot cross the border to the land of "Jimmy Carter and Mickey Mouse," he returns at the same time as his letter: the illusion is shattered because the problem must be solved here. A little optimistic poetry that prevents *Balconville* from turning into tragedy is suggested in the look Irene and Cecille cast at the stars, and in Irene's dream of the combat between Jacob and the angel, a projection towards a demonstratively mythical, non-realistic space. The steps too will be repaired, a small but important sign of amelioration, and the characters reveal a genuine sense of humour of their own.

In both plays, the street is an arena for public festivity. *Balconville* celebrates a folkloristic, yet rather self-conscious neighbourhood party:

– Where is everybody?
– This is it, we're all here.[18]

which turns into a fight. Levin's eight funerals can also be considered parties, in their grim humour and social atmosphere. The encounter of a character with his or her neighbor, even with the deceased him or herself, or at least with the next candidate for a funeral, is intended to reify the characters with their own justification for existence in the sense of "I am seen, therefore I am." The dramatis personae thus demonstrate to themselves their precise place in the hierarchy of suffering and humiliation, far beyond any class criteria. Such a degree of pessimism is neither desired nor achieved by Fennario's people. Real steps are built on Fennario's stage, but the drama transmits an egalitarian consciousness: Levin's play has an existential, hierarchical class consciousness, but everybody in it remains on the same physical plane and stage level.

The Crackwalker [19] (1980) by Judith Thompson (Canada) and Underground Waters [20] (1977) by Hillel Mittelpunkt (Israel) deal with people compared to whom the population of The Suitcase Packers and Balconville is rich, successful, and happy. In The Crackwalker there are five characters: Theresa, Sandy, Alan, Joe and a "man." Theresa is mentally handicapped, Joe and Alan steal motorcycle parts. The "man" is an Indian. The language in both plays is simple, aggressive and poetic, full of expressions connoting violent sexuality, expressed in implicity offstage action and explicit onstage behaviour. Pop music, rock and disco are used in ironic, sometimes poetical illumination of the mental state of the characters, their social onstage location and their psyches. So far, the plays are startingly alike. Both are harsh accounts of social and existential "miserables," whom they do not seem to judge or patronize.

In the Israeli play there are nine characters, most of them about the age of twenty, like the Canadians. Shaul is described as mentally handicapped. Miriam has a paralyzed leg. Some characters are homosexual, and others arrive on stage carrying stolen parts of vehicles. Da'ud is a thirty-year-old Arab. The location is a depressed area: "the edge of a swamp in the middle of a neighborhood. A high mound of sand and garbage rises near the swamp. The swamp itself, hidden from the eye, contains sewage, underground water, rain water, fluid wastes from a nearby beer factory. Abram's parents' house – a wooden table, three chairs, a television set. Eddie's shack – a straw mattress, two low stools. The time – the beginning of winter."

Plays concentrating on one or two families or on a small community, often propose to reveal an entire society in miniature. Speaking of her own play, Judith Thompson says: "I suppose the family is obviously a microcosm of how you relate to the whole world. People who have been able to manipulate their parents manipulate the world, and people for whom their parents were the ultimate authority tend to bow to other kinds of authority. The family is where I can really get in and study and investigate who people are."[21] Assuming that the small group expresses the greater conflicts of its broader social context, the playwright can describe tensions in the emotional and economic atmosphere of dependency in the family as a social microcosm, and so, under the magnifying glass, treat the problems of the macrocosm.

Two families, one with a baby, form the dramatic nucleus in *The Crackwalker*, while in *Underground Waters* there is one family and a few friends. Apart from the family, which represent the likelihood for understanding as well as for tragedy, there are two "strangers" in the plays: an Indian and an Arab, respectively, who emphasize the family's tension with the society around them. If the family itself is the society, who then is its enemy? Both Thompson and Mittelpunkt answer quite clearly: The Indian and the Arab. Da'ud, the Arab in the Israeli play, brings stolen goods on stage and does not gain the confidence of certain members of the group, who say: "Those guys, they would sell their own family" (while they themselves are doing the very same). Abram makes fun of Da'ud, calling him a Yemenite, a Kurd or some "other" kind of Jew whose standing on the social ladder is quite low. He "repatriates" the Arab Da'ud in an unconsciously ironical way, rather than admit his true ethnic origin. Later (scene 5), as a contemporary political hint, Da'ud himself says: "Now Beirut is no more" referring to the Lebanon War of 1981–3. Clinging to the lower rungs of the social ladder, Da'ud is made to say:

> The funniest thing is, there are some huge mice there . . . At night they think I'm asleep and they come to me from the water. And I . . . boom . . . smash their heads with a stone . . . so their heads explode on my clothes . . . There are my good pals, these mice, they make the night pass for me . . . [22]

Within the gloomy atmosphere of the play, Da'ud embodies (in a negative way) the national enmities represented through the social filter. He is not even called by his first by the other characters, only "The Arab," the main victim of the conflict. Mittelpunkt's depiction of him in a way resembles Thompson's of her Indian. Da'ud's lodgings reveal his status. He lives on the "other side" of the swamp together with the mice. The main message concerning the personage is transmitted through the shaping of his space rather than through his words.

"The Man" in *The Crackwalker*, the Indian, is open to both social and metaphysical interpretation, at least in the presentation of Jack Messenger, the director of the Israeli production of this Canadian play. The Indian appears on stage less frequently than Da'ud in *Underground Waters*, but his presence none the less hovers over the performance. He is a typical "silent character," a highly expressive and ominous "Cassandra-type," whose muteness absorbs social and psychological projections from all around. The Indian "lives" on the fringe of life and stage near the opening of a sewage pipe, and is an excellent stage representative for an offstage being, assuming that offstage in *The Crackwalker* is the realm of an overall deprivation.

The lives of the characters in these plays are described and presented rather than judged. The social context underlines the existential subtext. Thompson says that the girl Theresa, also an Indian, is not a victim. Hers is perhaps the Indian way to lose a baby, and yet accept the fact: " . . . There was a girl who was borderline mentally handicapped and she had this way of speaking and a wonderful purity about her . . . "[23] Although Theresa's being an Indian is mentioned only once, it suffices to denote the relationship between the "Indian inside" and the "Indian outside." Possibly the "Man" outside is indicative of the metaphysical realm, while Theresa represents the psychological and social one. In contrast the Arab character in *Underground Waters* has hardly any metaphysical overtones at all, except insofar as he appears as an abstract symbol of evil[24] within the society, because the Jewish poor and deprived perceive him so. Thompson's Indian has a more ominous presence because he is both external and closer to the onstage events.

Both plays are concentrated in a small, poor and highly "invaded" space, characterized by a deliberate lack of distinction between within and without. Thompson gives her characters (except for the Indian), a series of monologues, thus creating, for the length of the monologue, some sort of a private, common space with the audience. In both plays there are scenes in which the characters transgress the threshold between the inside and the outside spaces. In scenes 6 and 13 of *Underground Waters* there are demonstrative hesitations on the threshold and in scene 14 love-making occurs outside, on the verge of the swamp. Thompson too, and this is perhaps why *The Crackwalker* received unfavourable reviews, turns the inside out. Sandy, Joe, Theresa and Alan have no "inside" as a real space. They are a folk who live their inner spaces within themselves, on the street or in the house. The bourgeois notion that some things are "not done" outside does not apply to them: "Outside and inside are both intimate – they are always ready to be reversed, to exchange their hostility. If there exists a border-line surface between such an inside and outside, this surface is painful of both sides . . . The center of 'being there' wavers and trembles. Intimate space looses its clarity, while exterior space loses its void, void being the raw material of possibility of being. We are banished from the realm of possibility."[25]

Through Bachelard's words, one can understand something of the spatial milieu of the characters in both plays. The playwrights, through their use of space, deny the sense of privacy a person hopes to experience at home. In both plays strangers constantly enter their neighbor's house and behave in it as though it were their own. The invasion of privacy, the "confiscation" of home, results in the need to see one's immediate surroundings as a kind of extended home. Following "the territorial imperative,"[26] the characters would be expected to be either in their own spaces or in some public space rather than inhabiting another's space. It is reasonable to assume a direct connection between the kind of intimacy in the dialogue and the space in which the dramatic dialogue takes place, compatible with the intensity of the psychological exposure resulting from the encounter. Expressions such as: "I don't go back there," "Perhaps we'll leave," often appear in both plays, since the characters are doomed to a situation of exile even in the midst of a space allegedly belonging to them. Certainly the influence of the famous line from *Waiting for Godot* works here too, even though in less abstract formulations: " – Well? Shall we go? – Yes, let's go. (they do not move)." If the pattern of *Waiting for Godot* can be considered a centrifugal model fitting the Canadian situation, the pattern of *Endgame* is centripetal and no less lethal: "I'll leave you – You can't." and much more appropriate to the Israeli situation.

In the absence of psychological, economic and social security, the place itself, miserable as it may be, can still represent an odd compensation for other deprivations. Therefore the many violent invasions that the characters inflict on each other's space enhance the tension, but neither shatter the storyline nor bring about real action. Instead, the characters content themselves with sheer petty activity.

Abram in *Underground Waters* makes a vengeful speech about the housing projects inhabited by the kind of people who live in *Balconville* and *The Suitcase Packers*, which are erected right in front of his own shack. He wants to "attack the fences of the houses . . . blow up their cars . . . open the hoses . . . explode their ceramic tiles . . . their television sets . . . to scatter all they keep in their refrigerators . . . there will be a sea in the streets . . . pour gasoline on the sea and throw a match."[27] But it is again Abram who prevents Eddie from leaving, when the latter at least tries to change his oppressed fate. Abram is also one of the main oppressors in the play and his behavioral strategies are mostly territorial in nature.

In Joe's monology in *The Crackwalker* many "other" places which he has frequented are mentioned, but even Joe, who might have had a chance outside, returns to his own little swamp in the poverty-stricken neighbourhood in Kingston, Ontario. He has worked outside and made a lot of money, but he returns to his origins, his own security. Not love but the place itself draws him back. Alan, in a different and smaller variation on the same motif "flies out of the door" but later, in a beautiful stage repetition of the same "beat," is thrown out through an imaginary (or real?) door when he is fired. Deliberately or not, both men are given the same "spatial" destiny of "*Geworfenheit*," Heidegger's notion of the "*Condition Humaine*."

As a factor invading the imaginary space of the characters, it is interesting to note that television fulfils an important function in both plays. In both Israel and Canada (as can be observed in *Balconville* and *The Suitcase Packers* as well), television constitutes a very particular local universal world culture. Mittelpunkt and Thompson make good use of the added metaphorical value of the tube. As a substitute of life, television space invades not only peoples' private homes but the souls of the characters, deflecting them from even the small rebelliousness they might have mustered without it. In *The Crackwalker* the television inside the house is a sub-reality counterbalancing the symbolic (as well as real) super-reality of the Indian outside. Theresa is invited to choose between her "brothers" and television. Canadian ice-hockey can be seen as the social equivalent of soccer in Israel, as regards its place in popular consciousness. Abram, in trying to carry on a meaningful dialogue with his father, plucks the television wires from the wall, picks up the set, lets it fall and smashes it to smithereens. In this failure to unglue his father's eyes from the screen, he is emotionally right, of course, but his act does not bring about the longed-for dialogue. He wished to demolish the same television in his neighbors' houses, and now he simply does so in his father's.

A monstrous two-dimensionality may and indeed does ensue from this very matter. It is the similarity between the towns of Ramleh in *Underground Water* and Kingston in *The Crackwalker* that may arouse a real shudder, since it is the same music, the same television, the same clothes, the same urban alienation which bring about the inner alienation; electronic means of communication link flat and empty people who have no authentic spaces of their own. In this situation it is hardly surprising that the future is erased and that the babies in both plays are murdered by mistake, for the future holds no chances.

Both playwrights, with their credible descriptions of hopelessness, demand an immense amount of love and warmth from both actors and audience. Neither ending is happy or provides a solution. In Shakespearian plays, for instance, space as a central image of significance may grant at least a minimal amount of catharsis: Fortinbrass demands that the stage be cleared of all the dead at the end of *Hamlet*. In modern urban spaces the value of an external, religious and political lever is doubtful. Therefore a much higher degree of involvement and commitment is demanded of the audience itself, as occupying "the other side" of offstage. Perhaps unsurprisingly, the dialogue demanded by contemporary modes of forming dramatic spaces is not only aesthetic and artistic. It suggests the urgent need for inter-cultural dialogue, moving also in the direction of a moral stand and mutual responsibility between the stage and the auditorium, between the auditorium and the world around it.

6

Four Horsewomen of the Apocalypse

This chapter does not deal exclusively with drama, although Bejerano's piece is a play and Atwood's is a radioplay. It is intended to illuminate the comparison between Israeli and Canadian dramatic spaces from yet another angle. The four pieces discussed refer to "non-space," to U-Topos. I try to show that the descriptions of spaces that "have reached their end" in these apocalyptic works are strongly influenced by "normal" notions of space, Canadian or Israeli.

A Utopia is a plan for an ideal society which is basically different from known actuality, and embodying a moral, emotional, voluntary or utilitarian good. An anti-Utopia or a Distopia, on the other hand, is a description of an extremely negative society, equally non-existent, but intended to show Evil in the moral and emotional senses.[1]

In her study of Utopia Karin-Frank offers criteria such as order, descriptions of normal people, harmony, happiness and stability which are turned upside-down in a Distopia, where disorder or a negative and oppressive order take over. A "normal" person becomes unique by virtue of being able to observe the negative state of affairs, as a witness or even as a refugee from a more positive situation in the past. In a Distopia, the principal characteristics are arbitrariness, exploitation and wickedness. Disharmony replaces harmony – happiness turns into misery and stability is overturned by chaotic threats.

After two world wars, enormous technological development, the rise and fall of ideologies and regimes, universal ecological disasters and the horror of atomic destruction which could yet devastate the earth, twentieth-century art is characterized by an easily understandable revival of Utopias, Distopias and bitter attacks on Utopias and Utopianism.

From the many poems, plays, novels and short stories that variously express doomsday feelings and apocalyptic prophesies, I have chosen four works from different genres, presenting different approaches, by two Canadian and two Israeli writers.

The first is *Dolly City* (1992) by Orly Castel-Bloom (b. 1960),[2] a novel set in a Blade Runner, Los Angeles-like city of fallen and sick angels, where Dr Dolly lives and works as a physician who discovers radioactivity and cancer cells even on bus tires. She tries to immunize her baby son, whom she glues to her back, against all these horrors in a highly self-referential, self-ironizing and post-modernist text. The novel is considered one of the finest pieces of Israeli prose to have appeared in the past decade. The second piece is a *Poem for Voices*, "Oratorio for Sasquatch, Man and Two Androids" (1970) by Margaret Atwood (b. 1939),[3] a radio play that enlists Canadian mythology in the war against the destruction of nature. The invisible protagonist is the legendary Sasquatch, "maybe man's conscience." The third piece is Maya Bejerano's (b. 1949) poetic play *The Memorial Day Ceremony of the Paradisal City Tismit* (1986/7),[4] which although it resembles an ideological allegory is in fact a futuristic experiment in reconstructing the past as well as a double-edged fable: partly very local and partly universal and apocalyptic. The fourth and last work to be discussed is the centre-piece of P. K. Page's (b. 1916) collected volume *The Evening Dance of the Grey Flies*, the story "Unless the Eye Catch Fire . . . " (1981),[5] "which ostensibly deals with the death of earth as human habitation and the end of time as humanity dies; but on another level it projects a visionary perception, suggesting that one does not have to wait for the end of time to apprehend eternity."[6]

All four works have a dominant apocalyptic motif in common, which is approached here from different angles: *Dolly City* as seen primarily by its critics; *Tismit* as seen by the author in a special interview; Atwood's radioplay according to the medium-oriented criteria of the art of radio and P. K. Page's story as a spiritual and visionary statement.

The Apocalypse of the "I" and the Deranged City

In two of the many interviews she has given Orly Castel-Bloom was asked about her concept of reality, since an apocalyptic perception of the world is quite noticeable in her first books (she has written

six to date). Of *Dolly City* she says: "Fairytales? I may do them
one day. Utopia . . . I keep poetic, utopian texts at home . . . about
a state of calm, from an imaginary point of view, in a world which
exists on an inexistent line . . . " (*Yediot Ahronot*, 5 August 1987).
On another occasion two years later she remarked that "there
is reality and there is yet another reality. The existence of the
inner reality becomes stronger . . . I always check my concept of
reality."

Dolly City denies "all illusion of depth – in language, culture,
human experience, in the soul of private people, society, tradition,
the past. Castel-Bloom sees before her a reality that is composed
of a thin, shallow, tasteless, hardened and dead everyday automatic existence and a pit of chaos underneath it . . . " (Miron, *Al
Hamishmar* 16 June 1989). The novel excels in nihilistic despair to
such an extent that it reflects a kind of disappointed religiosity:
why does God not act against this miserable state of affairs? But
this may also be the reason why man must bear the responsibility
for destroying whatever needs destruction without assuring any
constructive alternative.

There are no redeeming, consoling features in Castel-Bloom's
apocalypse. The book opens with the dissection of a goldfish "until
I turned its body into millimetre thick little strips" (p. 9) and already
here a kind of echo, a vocal shadow, takes over the voice of Dolly,
the eponymous protagonist, a physician who, like a writer, dissects
and analyzes everything she encounters; her adopted son included.
At the end of the first chapter there appears a "vision of dry bones
of meaning, and at the end of this part, among the most ingenious
writing in Hebrew literature, the reader encounters a vision in the
fullest and most ancient sense of the word" (Hirschfeld, *Haaretz*, 29
May 1992).

In the meantime Dolly carves "Israel's map on my baby's back,
as I remembered it from biblical times . . . and drew with the blade
the sea of Galilee that spills into the Dead Sea that evaporates
non-stop . . . at long last I felt that I was cutting into the living
flesh . . . " (p. 29). This political satire is effective here only as far
as the shocking effect of the image lasts, but it is reflected again
in the third part of the book where Dolly is promised her son back
only if she "returns to the borders of 1967."

Notwithstanding such obviously political hints, *Dolly City* is not
a political novel at all, but uses local materials in the way glass
splinters are used in a (self-reflective!) kaleidoscope: Dolly is in

Dolly City as much as her son is "in Israel" that is also carved onto his back. Inside and outside are reversible.

Dolly City, with its repulsive, sick and hostile world, not only presents the apocalypse, but also activates "that which has been destroyed, changed and lost" (Hirschfeld, ibid.). Castel-Bloom does not try to imitate Orwell's Nineteen Eighty-four, for Dolly City is a democracy. Rather, she describes the two parties, Bureaucracy and Procedure, which together are in fact as powerful as a dictatorship, although they are vaguely portrayed as being beyond good or evil.

"The shifts between a hallucinated and a quasi real world turn the story into a saga, a myth, a kind of primary text, perhaps even biblical, the apocalyptic atmosphere of which is not only an external shell but an integral part . . . Dolly is a marionette, a hollow figure without an inside or an outside, a dust of a person. It is difficult to identify with her while at the same time it is not easy to reject her . . . "[7] The apocalypse of Dolly is that of a woman-city and there is a certain identity between the two.[8] In fact, the image of a woman-city is the opening symbol of Lamentations: "How doth the city sit solitary . . . she weepeth sore in the night, and her tears are on her cheeks; among all her lovers she hath none to comfort her; all her friends have dealt treacherously with her, they are become her enemies." This is the central metaphor that hovers above Dolly City.

Dolly, who dwells in the city as a semi-living consciousness, is certainly reminiscent of Doeblin's Berlin and Joyce's Dublin. But instead of either biblical prophesies of wrath and pathos or, alternatively, modernist streams of consciousness, Castel-Bloom uses a series of disseminated, highly sharpened and often unrelated images, in Hebrew street language purified of emotion. Her style is a sequence of "real" horror ridden video-clips mixed with internalized hallucinations in which each new violent image neutralizes the previous no less violent one. As is often the case in the medium of television, the readers of Dolly City are not given any time to digest. They are forced to choose between cringing with fear or letting increasing anxiety turn them numb and indifferent.

Castel-Bloom describes her characters analytically. Dolly sees sickness all around her like a mental cancer but rather than exploit the metaphor, the author develops the images ad absurdum and never asks whether life should be evaluated against the Socratic notion of "the good life." At the end of part two Dolly asks

Gordon: "Why don't you build yourself a ghost city?" but he, after half an hour of reflection, only repeats the question. "Maybe you don't want to build a ghost city but a ghost village?" Dolly City is an international, polluted, loud megalopolis "bottomless, past-less, structureless. A city where peoples' parts are connected to each other with associative links . . . "

Castel-Bloom shatters a number of Israeli taboos such as the sanctity of the Holocaust and the solemnity of bereavement for war casualties. As two "events" in Israeli–Jewish history, these two filters of Israeli identity have naturally been the foci of many satires and parodies (most of them politically oriented) but Castel-Bloom exposes the non-committed aspects of sheer ruthlessness. Her self-referential apocalyptic text is therefore meant to extricate the writer from her inferno through the very act of writing. Consequently, the reader is left with the uneasy task of supplying sense and significance where there are, perhaps, none. Responding to a question about the meaning of the coming of the Messiah, Castel-Bloom says: "The resurrection of the dead, that wars will stop, that people won't starve to death, that the wicked cease making money while the poor are getting poorer. Don't call it religiosity. It isn't that. It's a metaphysical matter, a human wondering in the limited framework of what Life means" (Dalia Carpell, an Interview with Orly Castel-Bloom in *Ha'ir*, 22 May 1987). *Dolly City* is indeed an expression of extreme wondering. It is, however, not an answer, for anxiety is petrifying, not redeeming.

The Apocalypse of Self and Nature

"Oratorio for Sasquatch, Man and Two Androids" is a *Poem for Voices*, a relatively less known piece by Margaret Atwood, which, thanks to the medium, invites more active participation from listeners than a film or a theatre play, because they must use the auditory signs and "direct" them visually within their minds.

"Sasquatch," "a subject of many Indian legends – perhaps myth" – has been lurking "blurred near the edges of jerky films," as the opening of the radioplay says. It is a hybrid creature (rather like the Himalayan Yeti, the Abominable Snowman), between man and animal, a primordial natural force, a blend of the enchantment and awe that people feel towards nature's creations. He is an "Adam Kadmon" (in the Kabbalistic sense), utterly at one with his surroundings, organically part of the trees and mountains, water and weather. In his radiophonic metamorphosis in Atwood's play, he presents a near-future revenge against those who are destroying his and their own natural surroundings. In medieval times sylphs and gnomes, nymphs and dwarfs were imaginative embodiments of the mystical, holistic and organic perception of nature. These creatures were humanoid expressions of the mineral, etheric and astral forces that humanity perceived in rocks, plants and animals. They were thought to be completely in harmony with their own particular climate and habitation for as long as people still dwelt less aggressively within the surrounding world. In modern Canada, where woods are systematically chopped down, lakes polluted, the earth poisoned and the air filled with smoke, Sasquatch is presented by Atwood as the eco-mythical voice of warning – "maybe man's conscience"?

Sasquatch appears here only vocally, and as a metaphorically-used legendary figure. This quality of vocal consciousness fits him well; he can be fleshed out in the listener's own imagination. He appears only at the beginning and the end of the radioplay, as though he were the Alpha and Omega of the entire auditory world portrayed in the piece. Throughout the poem he absorbs the opinions and feelings, projections and hopes of the male character and his two androids who try both to encounter and to flee him. This is a quest play in which a man tries with the help of two sub-human androids to find the super-human Sasquatch.

The space of every radioplay is, as Atwood is aware, the space of the imagination: "He cannot be read / he can only be heard / because he has no language / he speaks to each man in his own language. / The syllables are within you" (pp. 16–17). Atwood appeals to the auditory channel of perception, and challenges listeners to activate both their imagination and their consciousness.

The "Oratorio" is set in modern times and is no less relevant than when it was first written in 1970. At the same time, due to the radiogenic qualities of the piece, it can make use of cyclical and even a-temporal patterns as well as the simple linear ones. Although radio "time" – like music – is necessarily linear, beginning at a given hour and ending so many minutes later, the repetition of motives suggests a cyclical pattern of seasons as in the "natural" time of birth, death and new plant life. If humankind will continue to destroy all life with its invasive techniques of "(1) power (2) fame (3) money," time itself will come to an end for human beings.

The story line develops towards the Man's meeting with Sasquatch, leaving the two androids behind. While he retains his humanity, the two androids, who also appear to have encountered Sasquatch, react according to their technologically conditioned characters. The Quest for Sasquatch is a search for the human, a reconciliation with nature and an acceptance of the divine. Atwood implies that Sasquatch is the original human element in man, and as such – close to nature and the godly, even in the biblical sense.

Of the Androids one is "plated with flags – with badges; my eyes are gold buttons . . . ," and otherwise replete with symbols of the idol Mammon. He is the soaring, presumptuous embodiment of power-stricken Man, the Android who like the rebellious angel strikes the hawk in the sky and is associated with the "Fall." He seeks "power, fame and money." In his fear of Sasquatch he likens him, as in a fairytale, to the blind rage of a bear. Android 1 looks for Sasquatch "near the edge of jerky films," wants to give Sasquatch a name, define him, measure him. He represents the linear, precise aspect of a soul-bereaved technology. This Android too does not use his "real," namely spiritual eyes, and hence "insight" becomes mere "sight." He wants to explain nature away, fix it, nail it down and make it functional, ordered in lines. Rather like Goethe's Humunculus in *Faust*, he too is placed within a glass bubble and in his fear, imagines Sasquatch to be an enormous man; namely, that which he himself is not.

These two "extensions" of what is truly human emphasize that being human entails having spiritual, rather than material qualities. The play is a fable about losing one's soul by exploiting nature. The Androids are deaf and blind to what Atwood conceives as human and, indeed, on his way to meet Sasquatch, Man leaves his two inhuman "skins" behind and goes alone to the meeting, like Jacob about to wrestle with the angel. Whereas in the Bible the angel gives Jacob the name Israel, here it is Man who names Sasquatch.

The end of the piece is clearly Christological: Sasquatch suffers wounds in his green flesh like Jesus on the cross and Man's blood is spilled on the earth while he "himself" will soon be carried upward to a celestial kingdom. Salvation and resurrection may be found, Atwood suggests, through harmony with nature, a harmony of humankind with its true spiritual self.

This particular apocalypse is presented as an ecological threat, taking the place of a Christian cycle of Fall and Redemption.

The Apocalypse of a Society at Play

The Memorial Day Ceremony of the Paradisal City Tismit by Maya Bejerano is a play in twenty-five scenes with thirteen characters, eleven of whom return to Tismit, a town on the Mediterranean coast at the edge of a desert. Only the insane prophetess of the town is at home in the ruins of Tismit. Alex is a Bedouin; seven other characters are given names, four more are, respectively, a citizen, a woman worker, a boy and a girl. One may assume that the numeral groupings of 13, 12 and 7 refer to ancient Jewish magical numbers and are not accidental: they deepen the mythologically associative layers of the work.

Tismit was destroyed in an earthquake and when the original inhabitants wanted to return, they found strangers occupying their land. War breaks out and as a result the city is now completely ruined by hatred and pain. The few survivors disperse, but in due course they gather together once more to look for their town and hold a memorial day ceremony on its ruins. The play concentrates on the final ceremony and shows the inability of the group of young people to bear the weight of past memories.

The analogy with the history of Yamit, an Israeli town at the northern end of the Sinai Peninsula that was evacuated and totally destroyed by the army just before the territory was handed back to the Egyptians as part of the peace treaty, is certainly prominent, but obviously does not exhaust the meaning of the piece. Bejerano delineates another, much broader analogy with Israel as a whole, as a second circle of meaning around the occurrences on stage. The earthquake is an image representing the historical events that destroyed the ancient Kingdom of Israel; the Arabs are therefore "the strangers" and the Jews are the memory and ceremony-beridden inhabitants who come to try to settle again. The writer constructs her poetic drama on the well-known Israeli pattern of pioneering and revival plays only in order to insert a gloomy futuristic element of failure: resettlement is impossible. The future of the State of Israel is precarious. However, the play contains yet a third level, of universal apocalypse.

Whereas the first level of interpretation attracts an Israeli audience because of the immediate associations with the trauma of Yamit (and soon with the need to evacuate even more of the occupied territories), the second level is more ominous. The (so-called) national Hebrew poet, Haim Nachman Bialik, wrote a poem called *The Dead of the Desert* (Heb.: "metei midbar"), one interpretation of which sees the awakening of the dead in the poem as the Zionist undertaking doomed to be covered by the sands of the desert. Following this line, Bejerano implies that neither Time nor Space are the dominant factors in the "revival attempts," but Action. "For years they have been sleeping," say Bialik and Bejerano, and in both works the past emerges like the dead of the desert; sleep is very long and the awakening short and painful.

Bejerano's language is modern, charged with images and illusions and uneven insofar as it mixes various levels to fit the different characters. She moves from everyday prose to popular songs, shifts between her own poetry and a high biblical pathos. The use of many different levels of Hebrew endows the play with epic as well as lyrical features.

The set depicts a coastal ruin on the edge of the desert, sand dunes, scorching heat and three palm trees on the horizon. Near the ruin old pieces of furniture lie scattered about and indeed the first "dialogue" in the play takes place between the modern equipment brought by the youngsters – sun shades, water bottles and tools – and the old half-buried objects that have been lying there for many years.

In a recorded interview with Maya Bejerano (20 March 1994) she says that one of the options for the play's opening scene was the landing of a helicopter from which a woman archeologist would emerge, as a reminder of a "higher world than ours." Tismit, she adds, is not connected temporally to any specific time or space except the sea, which functions on a mythical level. Only the prophetess, a Cassandra-like figure, has another type of consciousness in the visions she sees and the voices she hears. Physical materials change form in the play, says Bejerano, order falls apart and half-experienced hallucinations of sand, blood and animal hair float and surge.

Bejerano defines "apocalypse" as the end of the world, that which lies before and after historical time. The play deals with suspended time and was written in "an atmosphere of dusk." It has a certain unity of time, but the logic that guides it is the logic of a ritual, a ceremony. It is, she says, a kind of game with its own independent reasoning; in a ceremony you can do what you want. "You decide your own limits and make space for freedom. You evoke associations and condensed, mixed experiences. The utopian dimension of Tismit is perhaps a mental state. Utopia can be found in the soul of every moral person and in Tismit an attempt is made to touch good and evil, the desired and the unwanted and harmful." Tismit is a cycle, a quest, a yearning for comfort. "Finally," says Bejerano, "we are left with the natural, flowing life instinct, not so much philosophy. We came to play, have some good times, not to philosophize about life."

"I," says Bejerano, "have had a love affair with Nature as an enormous lover; let it touch us in the cold, the heat, the rough and the pleasant; and this is how my characters in the play must act on the beach, undress and expose themselves. In an urban civilization this has no place. Yes, a kind of nudism, counterbalanced with the logic of a city, of consumerism, class, entertainment and establishment. In nature you look for balance."

Rebuilding the city of Tismit is a Utopian plan meant to maintain happiness for the individual, a formula to balance a child-like paradise with the established hierarchy and a heavy set of burdening images. This is why Tismit is near the sea. It is a city and yet not a city. Everyone there knows everybody else and the doors are always open. The people of Tismit are representatives of a much larger group that exists only in the collective memory. Every character carries within his or her self dozens of others. They are a group of individualists with a rich feeling for the beauty and strength of the body. They want to merge with something greater than themselves and join wider forces. A super-settlement, perhaps in space.

Tismit is also the wish to revive optimistic forces from the past. It is not "holy" in itself. It is in fact quite ordinary but it becomes special [in Hebrew "special" and "holy" are semantically quite close] because people come and sanctify it. but this is secular holiness, closer to the sanctity sought by Brenner and A. D. Gordon.[9]

Bejerano's text is partially based on the well-known Israeli "Hevre" notion, meaning "the group," usually a set of people with whom one grew up or joined in a kibbutz, a youth movement or in the army. This very characteristic Israeli ambiance has produced the material for anumber of "Hevre" plays, such as *Hevraya* by Itamar Ben Hur (1942), *The Night of the Twentieth* by Yehoshua Sobol (1976) and *Hevre* by Hanan Peled (1988). Ben Hur's play revolves around the mutual yearning for love and friendship between the members, and the utopian element is actually brought to a functional level: "As long as there is tomorrow, there is no despair. Faith in tomorrow is the shield against desperation" (p. 45). In *The Night of the Twentieth* tension arises between the goals of the group and the personal inclinations of the individuals in it, but the group is presented as strong because of – and not despite – the individuality of its members. However, this is a play towards a possible utopia, not a utopian play. Even less utopian is Peled's Hevre, an ironical drama about a neo-pioneering Utopia, abused by an Israeli arms dealer who escapes Interpol by enticing his "Hevre" to start a new, "clean, pure" settlement in Galilee in the late 1980s.

In comparison with these, *Tismit* – the name suggests an Assyrian or Babylonian origin – is indeed an attempt to present the utopian aesthetic of dreamers who do nothing and do not seem to intend any real action. They yearn to act, and do act, but in a dreamy state, rejecting the reality they encounter because of fear and weakness. The new settlers of Tismit ignore the "real" events of their ruined city and prefer to turn the past into a series of ceremonies; games which demand less commitment than the historical facts in the drama. The youngsters of Tismit want to remain forever young and beautiful and are ready to sacrifice reality for the sake of eternalizing their dreamy games. In this sense, *The Memorial Day Ceremony of the Paradisal City Tismit* is a self-destroying Utopia, since the "believers" never really intended to bring it about. They only wanted to play a little. They are the modern "Dead of the Desert," bereft of purpose and left only with empty ceremonies.

The Apocalypse of the Spiritual Self

P. K. Page's novella "Unless the Eye Catch Fire . . . " challenges the "end" from the point of view of a lonely woman who documents the last days of human existence on earth. The time is the continuous present of the act of writing, and the place is a West Canadian city (Vancouver?). The story line develops from a slight worry to the ineluctable certainty that everything, the whole world, will indeed catch fire.

Throughout the story, the notions of time and space undergo perceptual and conceptual changes, at least in the narrator's depiction of the events, and perhaps in the objective world too: finally the two are described as one. First the narrator's world changes over tiny sequences of time, space and the "other" consciousness are only adumbrated, presented as indescribable according to the notions acquired by humanity: "Inner and outer are the same. A continuum . . . We move to a higher water" (p. 60).

The simple plot takes place in a house with a garden outside the big city. Both house and garden are protected locations. Later the house will be treated with foam against the growing heat. A growing identity develops between the house and the narrator, until the house becomes a metaphor (not unexpectedly) for the human body: "we are one, the house and I" – parts of some vibrating sensitive metonymy for the relationship between humanity and nature.

The garden in *Unless the Eye Catch Fire* is a "real place" as well as a meeting space between wild, uncontrollable and indifferent nature on the one hand and man's little agricultural needs and deeds on the other. The garden enables a certain control over nature, a miniature dialogue where people may witness and influence natural processes of growth and decay. Gardening gradually becomes more difficult, then impossible. Page alludes delicately to Voltaire's "Cultiver son jardin," implying that this can no longer serve as a real or metaphorical option at the dying end of the twentieth century, especially because of ecological disasters. Now the world reveals its holistic, organic nature and the (allegedly) redeeming "gardening" deeds of the individual have only an inner meaning, no longer a practical one. In the beginning the garden was a kind of Garden of Eden. Then came the "Efficient, noisy desecrators of my twenty years of landscaping . . . " who turned the garden into a soy bean plantation, "rich with the promise of protein" (p. 48). The twenty years of gardening were a harmonic, fruitful encounter between humanity and nature, rich with tender loving care rather than "protein." Though Page does not elaborate on this issue, it is quite clear that she accuses "improvident, greedy mankind – whose polluted, strike-ridden world is endangered now by the fabled flames of hell" (p. 47).

One of the images intended to bridge the gap between the need and the wish to describe "what is beyond description?" (p. 58) is expressed in the words There and Here. Only one letter differentiates between them.

Time too loses its habitual grip over reality. The entries in the narrator's diary begin with "September 17," "Wednesday," followed by indications of the month only, then "some time later" and "who knows how much later" until "The end." The documenting dates of this apocalypse are gradually blurred since time becomes more subjective while reflecting through its subjectivity the actual flow of events. Time itself, like space, fades away, leaving colors instead. The past is no longer relevant: "At first it was interesting to see how quickly drugs, pollution, education, women's lib., all became by-gone issues . . . " (p. 48). Yet later the future merges into the present, as into the past, and loses its "future" quality since "Because there is no expectation, there is no frustration" (p. 60). Certainly, the collapse of Time has a "realistic" justification in the story's fictional world, because in times of stress people tend to focus on the immediate. On a more basic level, the reader learns that together with the dying world, the major notions with which we try to grasp this world also die.

Most of the means of communication that appear in "Unless the Eye Catch Fire" such as radio, mail, telephones, vehicles etc. are traditionally perceived as inter-connecting people's times, spaces and consciousness. Because of the heat, these means fail technically. But Page shows how the main message of "the end" could not have passed through them in any case, since it is a spiritual one. Radio, newspapers and the like can only hint that another, non-transferable meaning is "there," and indeed only a "chosen" but growing number of "shake-freaks" – those who have experienced "the changes" and the colors that always occur with a tremor – can decipher the message. Those who know are the driver Ballantyne, a Mrs Howard, Sydney the garage attendant. A pact is created among these knowers of the secret, the "shake-freaks" who are drawn to each other, the ones who "understand the colors" and they are in no need of any further information beyond the (religious) self-evidence of the experience itself:

> "'Do you know anyone else?' I said.
> 'One or two. Three, actually. Do you?'
> I shook my head. 'You are the first. Is it . . . Is it . . . always like that?'
> 'You mean . . . ?' he gestured towards his heart."

Page describes an experience that mystics and scholars of religion (William James, Otto, Scholem) have found difficult if not impossible to portray. "There didn't seem anything more to talk about. Your right hand hasn't much to say to your left, or one eye to the other. There was comfort in the experience, if comfort is the word, which it isn't. More as if an old faculty had been extended. Or a new one activated."

She employs a number of religiously-charged expressions and in fact describes an epiphany, a transfiguration. She uses the classical elements of earth, water and air, all of which are tested by the fourth element, fire, that gives light and heat inasmuch as it burns and kills. Light and destruction are one in the same way that the "I" and the world unite. The world, according to Page's precise and frightening techno-modern image, is a "self-cleaning oven." A mythological "external" inferno is superfluous. Destruction and resurrection are built into a holistic world.

"Unless the Eye Catch Fire" is a story of a major change that cannot be fully explained, for lack of adequate notions that are obviously part of the change itself. Between what is self-evident to some and inexplicable to others, Page uses "The colors" as the main image. In them, matter undergoes a process of spiritualization. The colors exist beyond light and darkness and "all comparisons were prevented by the startling infinities of darkness and light" (p. 40). Through "the colors" seeing itself changes, and Page may have alluded to Goethe's words about the eye that cannot see without having something of the sun in itself. The reader is directed towards an organic, mystical and qualitative consciousness by the shedding of the quantitative "scientific" mode. The mystical union is possible, Page says, when subject and object become one: "I not only saw but actually was the two spectrums" (p. 40) that are life giving.

The beauty of material annihilation and death as a passage to higher levels of being is exquisitely portrayed in images referring to the earth as a child in fever, a wild animal and especially in the description of the dog Dexter's merciful death. His glowing body . . . "In that dazzling, light filled moment . . . like those from which saints receive revelations . . . " (p. 60) is reminiscent of biblical scenes such as Elijah's ascent to heaven and the death of Mary.

In addition to the intensive use of the four elements, Page follows a quasi-medieval world order in her descriptions of the mineral, the vegetal, the animal and the human spheres. Having treated the plant world thoroughly, she uses the life and death of the dog as a metaphor (and not a metaphor . . .) for the sanctity of life as such. The narrator loves him dearly; he is the only physical contact in her lonely house and his death is the only one described directly in this story about dying. Dexter's death finishes off, so to speak, not only the ethereal but also the astral level of being. But "Then a great peace filled me – an immense space, light and sweet – and I realized that this was death . . . I contained him . . . " (p. 58). Sorrow does not pass immediately because "the flesh forgets slowly" (p. 59). Page does not supply the reader with facile spiritual solutions.

In this sense too she walks the tightrope between matter-of-fact realistic writing and visionary ramifications that grow more explicit towards the end of the world and of the story.

In the end, some of the opening images receive, retrospectively, additional power, like the flock of birds that soar diagonally upward, as though sucked up. Then "the merest shake occurred – moireed the garden – rectified itself." Seeing in "Unless the Eye Catch fire" necessitates a passage to another level of reality, a turning to the inner eye that catches fire.

The major difference that can be detected between these four apocalypses, setting aside the obvious personal emphases on medium, genre and style, relates to the historical versus the geographical perception. "The End," according to Atwood and Page, is "space-oriented," linked with alienation from nature and conceived through an ecological disaster. The city, in both *Sasquatch* and *Unless the Eye Catch Fire* is remote, and the action takes place either far away from it or among the woods.

The Israeli perspective of the apocalypse according to Bejerano and Castel-Bloom is not only much more time-bound than in the Canadian works, but it focuses on a city. Even Tismit, a ruined city on the edge of the desert and the sea, is an attempt to relocate the protagonists in an urban (at least semi-urban) human habitation.

Furthermore, the basic experiences treated in these works are group experiences on the Israeli side, and profoundly individual on the Canadian. Writing about the universally perceived limits of time, space and human consciousness must pass through local, specific "filters" of climate, cultural environment and personal up-bringing. Here the two Canadian writers seem to balance their sense of the end against the immense Canadian space surrounding them, whereas the Israeli horsewomen of the apocalypse harness their steeds to an historical notion of civilization, reconstructed or totally deformed. Outside the Israeli mental garrison the end appears as "no more time," while for the Canadian there is "no more space left."

Notes

Introduction

1. Pierre Berton, *Why We Act Like Canadians* (Toronto, McClelland and Stewart, 1986), p. 130.
2. Jerry Wasserman (ed.), *Modern Canadian Plays* (Vancouver, Talon Books, 1985), p. 12.
3. *Tsomet Hasharon* (newspaper), 11 May 1990.
4. Northrop Frye, *The Great Code* (Toronto, Academic Press Canada, 1982), p. 218.
5. Denis Silk, *Retrievements* (Jerusalem, Keter, 1969), p. 9.
6. Berton, *Why We Act Like Canadians*, p. 119.
7. Percy Rowe, *Travel Guide to Canada* (Mackham, Ont., Paperjacks, 1977).
8. Grey Owl, *The Men of the Last Frontier* (Toronto, Macmillan of Canada, 1931), p. 1.
9. Berton, *Why We Act Like Canadians*, p. 119.
10. Yehuda Sommo, *The Comedy of Betrothal* (ed. J. Schirman) (Tel Aviv, Tarshish-Devir, 1965).
11. Wasserman, *Modern Canadian Plays*, p. 9.
12. Richard Plant, L. W. Conolly, "Drama in English." James Noonan, Louise Forsyth, "Drama in French," both in William Toye (ed.), *Oxford Companion to Canadian Literature* (Toronto, Oxford University, 1983), pp. 192–213.
13. Wasserman, *Modern Canadian Plays*, p. 12.
14. Howard Fink with Brian Morrison, *Canadian National Theatre on the Air 1925–1961* (Toronto, University of Toronto Press, 1983).
15. See Ladislav Matejka and Irwin R. Titunik (eds), *Semiotics of Art* (Cambridge, Mass., MIT Press, 1976); and Keir Elam, *The Semiotics of Theatre and Drama* (London Methuen, 1980).
16. Northrop Frye, Conclusion to "A Literary History of Canada" in *The Bush Garden. Essays on the Canadian Imagination* (Toronto, Anansi, 1971), p. 225.

17. Amos Elon, *The Israelis* (Tel Aviv, Shochen, 1972), pp. 283–92.
18. Robert Wallace, "Writing the Land Alive," in Anton Wagner (ed.), *Contemporary Canadian Theatre* (Toronto, Simon & Pierre, 1985), p. 80.

Chapter 1   Offstage: Space as a Present Void

1. Following Wolfgang Iser, *The Implied Reader* (Baltimore, Johns Hopkins University Press, 1974).
2. Austin Quigley, *The Modern Stage and Other Worlds* (New York, Methuen, 1985), p. 45.
3. Peter Brook, *The Empty Space* (Atheneum, New York, 1968).
4. Quigley, *The Modern Stage*, p. 24.
5. J. Honzl, "Dynamics of the Sign in the Theatre," in L. Matejka and J. R. Titunik (eds), *Semiotics of Art* (Cambridge, Mass., MIT Press, 1976), pp. 74–5. ". . . although the stage is usually a construction, it is not its constructional nature that makes it a stage but the fact that it *represents* dramatic place." As explained here, I expand the term *offstage*, beyond its technical ramifications, as, for instance in Katharine Worth, "Space and Sound in Beckett's Theatre," in Kate Worth (ed.), *Beckett the Shape Changer* (London, Routledge and Kegan Paul, 1975), p. 186: ". . . the impression of an off-stage area that infinitely extends the bareness and emptiness, and multiplies the opportunities for wandering freely . . . "
6. Ludwig Wittgenstein, *Tractatus Logico-Philosophicus* (London, Routledge and Kegan Paul, 1960), p. 188.
7. Freddie Rokem, "Stage Space and the Fictional World in Modern Theatre" (in Hebrew), *Aley Sia'ch*, vol. 19 / 20, p. 333ff.
8. Victor Turner, *From Ritual to Theatre* (New York, Performing Arts Journal Publications, 1982). In the chapter "Liminal to Liminoid" Turner distinguishes between his own "comparative symbology" and the semiotic and semiological approach. As an anthropological-performative method, Turner's approach is helpful in this context. See also: Mircea Eliade, *Shamanism* (Princeton, New Jersey, 1972). Manfred Krueger, *Wandlungen des Tragischen, Drama und Initiation* (Stuttgart, Logoi, 1973), p. 25ff.
9. Richard Hornby, *Drama, Metadrama and Perception* (Lemisbury, Pa., Bucknell University Press, 1986), p. 31ff.
10. S. Lieberman and F. J. Miller (eds), *Roman Drama* (New York, Bantam, 1964), p. 374.
11. Anne Ubersfeld, "The Space of Phedre," *Poetics Today* (1980), vol. 2, no. 3, p. 209.
12. E. K. Chambers, *The Medieval Stage* (Clarendon, 1903). See also: Oscar G. Brockett, *The Essential Theatre* (New York, Holt Rinehart and

Winston, 1984); A. M. Kinghorn, *Medieval Drama* (London, Evans, 1968).

13. Leon Moussinac, *Le Theatre* (Ranz, Flammarion, 1966) (Hebrew version, Tel Aviv, Dvir, 1966), p. 32.

14. Arthur O. Lovejoy, *The Great Chain of Being* (Cambridge, Mass., Harvard University Press, 1961).

15. Michael Issacharoff, "Space and Reference in Drama," *Poetics Today* (1980), vol. 2, no. 3, p. 212.

16. J. W. von Goethe, *Faust* (trans. A. G. Latham) (London, Dent, 1928), p. 18.

17. Tom Stoppard, *Rosenkrantz and Guildenstern are Dead* (London, Faber & Faber, 1967), p. 20.

18. Cf. Shimon Levy, *The Three I's: The Self Referential Drama of Samuel Beckett* (London, Macmillan, 1990), for a more extensive discussion of offstage.

19. Herta Schmid, *Strukturalistische Dramentheorie* Skripten 3 (Kronberg TS., Scriptor, 1973). I am here following Schmid's distinction between authorial [playwright's] text – i.e. stage directions – and dialogal text of the characters].

Chapter 2   Local and Universal Space

1. Clifford Geertz, *The Interpretation of Cultures* (New York, Basic Books, 1973) (p. 39 in the Hebrew version).

2. Martin Esslin, *The Theatre of the Absurd* (New York, Doubleday, 1969).

3. Anton Wagner, *Contemporary Canadian Theatre* (Toronto, Simon & Pierre, 1985), p. 18.

4. John Millington Synge, *Riders to the Sea*, in John Hampden (ed.) *Twenty One-Act Plays* (London, Dent, 1941).

5. Eugene Benson, *J. M. Synge* (London, Macmillan), p. 56.

6. Robin Skelton, *The Writings of J. M. Synge* (Indianapolis, Bobbs-Merrill Co.), p. 48.

7. Maurice Bourgeois, *John Millington Synge and the Irish Theatre* (New York, Haskell House, 1966), p. 163.

8. Myron Galloway, etc. in L. W. Conolly, *Canadian Drama and the Critics* (Vancouver, Talon Books, 1987), p. 120.

9. A. B. Yehoshua, *A Night in May* (Bimot, 1969) (in Hebrew).

10. Michael Cook, *The Head, Guts and Soundbone Dance* in Richard Perkyns (ed.), *Major Plays of the Canadian Theatre* (Toronto, Irwing, 1984), pp. 443–77.

11. Michael Cook, *Jacob's Wake*, in Jerry Wasserman (ed.), *Modern Canadian Plays* (Talon Books, Vancouver, 1985), pp. 215–48.

12. Wasserman, *Modern Canadian Plays*, p. 213.
13. Cook, *Jacob's Wake*, p. 215.
14. Ibid., p. 247.
15. Yehoshua, *A Night in May*, p. 116.
16. An interview with A. B. Yehoshua, N. Calderon and M. Perri, "To Write Prose," *Siman Keri'a* (1976), no. 5, p. 284.
17. And also: "Literature has a socio-psychological function to perform, a cathartic one, which lies first and foremost in the release of our repressions . . . " in Ehud Ben Ezer (ed.), *Unease in Zion* (Tel Aviv, Am Oved, 1986), p. 113. Cf. also: "On the outside Yehoshua adheres to the mode of the well made play . . . inwardly he prefers the layer that deals with the individual . . . in Hillel Barzel, "Pictorial Thinking," *Yedioth Ahronot*, February 1976. Nili Sadan-Loebenstein, *A. B. Yehoshua, A Monograph* (Tel Aviv, Sifriat Poalim, 1981, p. 29: ". . . In Yehoshua's plays the external, dramatic action is minimal; whereas the main weight lies in the mental, internal activity." (All citations in Hebrew).
18. Conolly, *Canadian Drama*, p. 127.
19. Wasserman, *Modern Canadian Plays*, p. 214.
20. Perkyns, *Major Plays*, p. 445.
21. II Kings, 2:11.

Chapter 3   Mythical Space, Pathos and Irony

1. See, for example, Hoelderlin, *Empedokles' Death*.
2. Merill Denison, "Nationalism and Drama," in Bertram Brooker (ed.), *Yearbook of the Arts in Canada, 1928–1929*.
3. Gideon Ofrat, *Earth, Man, Blood* (Tel Aviv, Gome-Cherikover, 1980), pp. 200–24 (in Hebrew).
4. S. Friedlander, *Nazism, An Essay on Kitsch and Death* (Jerusalem, Keter), p. 21 (in Hebrew).
5. D. Rubinstein, in his *The Fig Tree Embrace* (Jerusalem, Keter, 1990) describes the Palestinians' claim to their land as a national ritual. Plays that exemplify his argument (although they are not mentioned in his book, are *Jabar's Head* (Nazareth Theatre) and most productions of the Arab theatre in Jerusalem, Al Hakawati. See also Shimon Levy, "The 1988/9 Theatre Season in Israel," *Assaf*, no. 5, pp. 175–84.
6. Eliezer Schweid, *The One* [A. D. Gordon's World] (Tel Aviv, Am Oved, 1970), p. 170 ff.
7. Shin Shalom, *Adama* (manuscript).
8. Ibid.
9. Ofrat, *Earth, Man, Blood*, p. 128 ff. For comparison, see also Ehud Ben Ezer, *Breakthrough and Siege, Keshet*, 54, (1968). The author examines the

motif of the besieged space in Hebrew literature, *vis-á-vis* Arab-Jewish relationships. Haim Shoham, "Generation and Land–Man–Space Relationships in Israeli Drama," *Moznaim*, 46 (1978), pp. 408–14. I am indebted to H. Shoham for his insights.

10. Alexander Carmon, *Bonfires*, pp. 6–7.
11. "Shin" Shalom, *Collected Writings*, vol. 7 (Tel Aviv, Yavne), p. 180.
12. Moshe Shamir, *He Went in the Fields* (Tel Aviv, Or Am, 1989), p. 7 (in Hebrew).
13. Yig'al Mossinson, *In the Wastes of the Negev* (Tel Aviv, Or Am, 1989) (in Hebrew).
14. Nathan Shaham, *They'll Be Arriving Tomorrow* (Tel Aviv, Or Am, 1989) (in Hebrew).
15. Diane Bessai (ed.), *Prairie Performance* (NeWest Press, Edmonton, 1980), p. 176.
16. Herman Voaden, "Hill-Land," in Richard Perkyns (ed.), *Major Plays of the Canadian Theatre* (Toronto, Irwin Publishing, 1984), pp. 19–65.
17. Ahron Ashman, *This Land*, in *Plays* (Tel Aviv, Yessod, 1973), vol. 2.
18. Ofrat, *Earth, Man, Blood*, p. 80.
19. Conolly, *Canadian Drama*, p. 15.
20. Perkyns, *Major Plays*, p. 22.
21. Ofrat, *Earth, Man, Blood*, p. 82.
22. Perkyns, *Major Plays*, p. 23.
23. John Murrell, *Farther West* (Toronto, Coach House Press, 1985).
24. Yaakov Shabtai, *Spotted Tiger* (Tel Aviv, Hakibbutz Ha'Meuchad, 1985).
25. Eugene Ionesco, *The Chairs* (New York, Grove Press, 1958), pp. 111–60.
26. Urjo Kareda, An Introduction to Murrell, *Farther West*, p. 10.

Chapter 4 Oppressed Space

1. Gaston Bachelard, *The Poetics of Space* (Boston, Beacon Press, 1964), p. xxxi.
2. J. P. Sartre, *Les peintures de Giacometti (Situations)* (Tel Aviv, Hakibbutz Ha'Meuchad, 1984), p. 58.
3. Terry Goldie, "Fear and Temptation" in T. King, C. Calver and H. Hoy (eds), *The Native in Literature* (Toronto, ECW Press, 1987), p. 73.
4. Goldie, *The Native*, p. 67.
5. Margaret Atwood, *Survival* (Toronto, Anansi, 1972), p. 95.
6. Sartre, *Giacometti*, p. 36.
7. Margery Fee, "Romantic Nationalism," in *The Native . . .* , p. 30.
8. Amos Elon, *The Israelis* (New York, Bantam, 1972), p. 32.
9. Ehud Ben Ezer, "Breakthrough and Siege," *Keshet*, 54, (1968) (in Hebrew).

10. Wasserman, *Modern Canadian Plays*, p. 20.
11. Gideon Ofrat, "The Arab in Israeli Drama," *Jerusalem Quarterly* (1979), no. 11, p. 70. See also, Dan Orian, *The Arab in Israeli Theatre* (in press, in Hebrew).
12. Jamie Portman, in Conolly, *Canadian Drama*, p. 83.
13. Wasserman, *Modern Canadian Plays*, p. 26.
14. Whittaker, in Conolly, *Canadian Drama*, p. 139.
15. Friedman, in Conolly, *Canadian Drama*, pp. 141–3.
16. Shaham, ibid.
17. S. Yizhar, *The Prisoner*, in Joel Blocher (ed.), *Israeli Stories* (New York, Schocken, 1962).
18. Yizhak Laor, *Ephraim Returns to the Army* (Tel Aviv, Timon, 1987) (in Hebrew).
19. George Ryga, *Indian*, In Richard Plant, *Modern Canadian Drama* (Penguin Books, 1984), p. 152–74.
20. Robertson, in Conolly, *Canadian Drama*, p. 43.
21. Russell, in Conolly, *Canadian Drama*, p. 42.

Chapter 5   Presentations of Social Space

1. David Fennario, "Balconville," in Jerry Wasserman (ed.), *Modern Canadian Plays* (Vancouver, Talon Books, 1985), pp. 279–310.
2. Hanoch Levin, *The Suitcase Packers* (Tel Aviv, Hakibbutz Ha'Meuchad, 1988).
3. Fennario, "Balconville," p. 279.
4. Richard N. Coe, *The Theatre of Jean Genet* (New York, Grove Press, 1970), p. 89.
5. Levin, *The Suitcase Packers*, p. 348.
6. Shimon Levy, *The Three I's: The Self Referential Drama of Samuel Beckett* (London, Macmillan, 1990), p.48 ff.
7. Fennario, "Balconville," p. 295.
8. Susan Sontag, *Illness as Metaphor* (New York, Vintage Books, 1978).
9. Levin, *The Suitcase Packers*, p. 354.
10. Fennario, "Balconville, p. 309.
11. David Heyd, "Is Life Worth Reliving?," *Mind* (1983), vol. 93, pp. 21–37.
12. L. W. Conolly, *Canadian Drama and the Critics* (Vancouver, Talon Books, 1987), p. 237.
13. Boaz Evron, *Yedi'ot Ahronot*, 15 March 1983.
14. Conolly, *Canadian Drama*, p. 237.
15. Ibid., p. 234.
16. Ibid., p. 231.
17. Fennario, "Balconville," p. 288.

18. Ibid., p. 292.
19. Judith Thompson, *The Crackwalker* (Playwrights Canada, 1987).
20. Hillel Mittelpunkt, *Underground Waters* (Tel Aviv, Hakibbutz Ha'-Meuchad, 1979).
21. Judith Thompson, in an interview with Sandra Tomc, in *Canadian Theatre Review* (1989), no. 59, pp. 200ff.
22. Mittelpunkt, *Underground Waters*, p. 5.
23. CTR 59, p. 23, ibid. *Canadian Theatre Review* 59 (1989).
24. Gideon Ofrat, "The Arab in Israeli Drama," *Jerusalem Quarterly* (1979), no. 11, p. 90.
25. Bachelard, *The Poetics of Space*, p. 218.
26. The term is Robert Ardry's: *The Territorial Imperative* (London, Collins, 1970).
27. Mittelpunkt, *Underground Waters*, p. 25.

Chapter 6   Four Horsewomen of the Apocalypse

1. Shaili Karin-Frank, *Utopia Reconsidered* (Tel Aviv, Hakibbutz Hamechuad, 1986) (in Hebrew).
2. Orly Castel-Bloom, *Dolly City* (Tel Aviv, Zmora-Bitan, 1992) (in Hebrew).
3. Margaret Atwood, "Oratorio for Sasquatch, Man and Two Androids," in *Poems for Voices* (Toronto, Canadian Broadcasting Corporation, 1970).
4. Maya Bejerano, *The Memorial Day Ceremony of the Paradisal City Tismit* (Tel Aviv, Keter-Achshav, 1993) (in Hebrew).
5. P. K. Page, "Unless the Eye Catch Fire . . . " in *The Evening Dance of the Grey Flies*.
6. William Toye (ed.), *The Oxford Companion to Canadian Literature* (Toronto, Oxford University Press, 1983), p. 631; entry by George Woodcock.
7. Baruch Blich, "Dolly City, The Light of Generations," *Te'amim*, December 1993, pp. 26–7 (in Hebrew).
8. Motti Geiger, "The Mother, The Son and the Spirit of Postmodernism," *Zero-Two*, Winter 1993 (in Hebrew).
9. Two pioneers of the early years of Jewish settlement in Palestine. Brenner was a highly acclaimed author and Gordon a leading ideologist who put his teachings on simplicity, purity and spirituality achieved through hard physical labour into arduous practice.

Bibliography

Canadian Anthologies and Plays (Selected list)

Anthologies

1. Bessai, Diane (ed.), *Prairie Performance*, Edmonton, NeWest Press, 1980.
2. Perkyns, Richard (ed.), *Major Plays of the Canadian Theatre*, Toronto, Irwin Publishing, 1984.
3. Plant, Richard (ed.), *Modern Canadian Drama*, Toronto, Penguin Books, 1984.
4. Wagner, Anton (ed.), *Contemporary Canadian Theatre*, Toronto, Simon & Pierre, 1985.
5. Wasserman, Jerry (ed.), *Modern Canadian Plays*, Vancouver, Talon Books, 1985.

Plays Referred To

1. Cook, Michael, *The Head, Guts and Soundbone Dance* (in Perkyns); *Jacob's Wake* (in Wasserman).
2. Fennario, David, *Balconville* (in Waserman).
3. Murrell, John, *Farther West*, Toronto, Coach House Press, 1985.
4. Ryga, George, *Indian* (in Plant); *The Ecstasy of Rita Joe* (in Wasserman).
5. Thompson, Judith, *The Crackwalker*, Playwrights Canada, 1987.
6. Voaden, Herman, *Hill Land* (in Perkyns).

Plays Mentioned and/or Consulted

Coulter, *Riel*.
Herbert, *Fortune and Men's Eyes*.
Fruet, *Wedding in White*.
Freeman, *Creeps*.
French, *Of the Fields, Lately; Jitters*.

Reaney, *Handcuffs: The Donnellys pts I+II+III.*
Pollock, *Blood Relations; Walsh; Generations.*
Hollingsworth, *Ever Loving.*
Stratton, *Rexy!*
Ringwood, *Garage Sale; Drum Song; A Fine Colored Easter Egg; Maya.*
Walker, *The Art of War.*
Zastrozzi, *The Master of Discipline.*
Salutin, *1837: The Farmers Revolt; The Farm Show.*
Ritter, *Automatic Pilot.*
Gray & Peterson, *Billy Bishop Goes to War.*
Aviva Ravel, *Dispossessed.*
Bolt, *Buffalo Jump.*
Gelinas, *Bousille and the Just.*
Davies, *At My Heart's Core.*
Tremblay, *Forever Yours Marie Lou.*
Herschel Hardin, *Esker Mike and his Wife Agiluk, Drama Review* (1969), vol. 14.
Richard Krizane, *Tamara.*
Beissel, *Inook and the Sun.*

Secondary Sources

Ardrey, R., *The Territorial Imperative*, London, Collins, 1969.
Atwood, Margaret, *Survival*, Toronto, Anansi, 1972.
Bachelard, Gaston, *The Poetics of Space*, Boston, Beacon Press, 1969.
Beckett, Samuel, *Cascando*, London, Faber & Faber, 1986.
Benson, Eugene, *J. M. Synge*, London, Macmillan, 1982.
Berton, Pierre, *Why We Act Like Canadians*, Toronto, McClelland and Stewart, 1986.
Brockett, Oscar G., *The Essential Theatre*, New York, Holt Rinehart and Winston, 1984.
Brook, Peter, *The Empty Space*, New York, Atheneum, 1968.
Bourgeois, Maurice, *John Millington Synge and the Irish Theatre*, New York, Haskell House, 1966.
Chambers, E. K., *The Medieval Stage*, Clarendon, 1903.
Coe, Richard N., *The Theatre of Jean Genet*, New York, Grove Press, 1970.
Conolly, L. W., *Canadian Drama and the Critics*, Vancouver, Tolon Books, 1987.
Denison, Merill, "Nationalism and Drama," in Bertram Brooker (ed.), *Yearbook of the Arts in Canada, 1928–1929.*
Elam, Keir, *The Semiotics of Theatre and Drama*, London, Methuen, 1980.
Eliade, Mircea, *Shamanism*, Princeton, New Jersey, 1972.
Enzensberger, Hans Magnus, *Der Untergang der Titanic*, Tel Aviv, Sifriat Hapoalim, 1986 (Hebrew).

Esslin, Martin, *The Theatre of the Absurd*, New York, Doubleday, 1969.

Fink, Howard, with Brian Morrison, *Canadian National Theatre on the Air 1925–1961*, Toronto, University of Toronto Press, 1983.

Frye, Northrop, Conclusion to "A Literary History of Canada" in The Bush Garden. *Essays on the Canadian Imagination*, Toronto, Anansi, 1971.

Frye, Northrop, *The Great Code*, Toronto, Academic Press Canada, 1982.

Geertz, Clifford, *The Interpretation of Cultures*, New York, Basic Books, 1973.

Grey Owl, *The Men of the Last Frontier*, Toronto, Macmillan of Canada, Toronto, 1931.

Heyd, David, "Is Life Worth Reliving?" *Mind* (1983), vol. 92, pp. 21–37.

Honzl, J., "Dynamics of the Sign in the Theatre," in L. Matejka and I. R. Titunik (eds), *Semiotics of Art*, Cambridge, Mass., MIT Press, 1976.

Hornby, Richard, *Drama, Metadrama and Perception*, Lewisburg, Pa., Bucknell University Press, 1986.

Ionesco, Eugene, *The Chairs*, New York, Grove Press, 1958.

Iser, Wolfgang, *The Implied Reader*, Baltimore, Johns Hopkins University Press, 1974.

Issacharoff, Michael, "Space and Reference in Drama," in *Poetics Today* (1980), vol. 2, no. 3.

King, T., C. Calver and H. Hoy (eds), *The Native in Literature*, Toronto, ECW Press, 1987.

Kinghorn, A. M., *Medieval Drama*, London, Evans, 1968.

Krueger, Manfred, *Wandlungen des Tragischen, Drama und Initiation*, Stuttgart, Logoi, Verlag Freies Geistesleben, 1973.

Levy, Shimon, *The Three I's*, London, Macmillan, 1990.

Levy, Shimon, "The 1988/9 Theatre Season in Israel," in *Assaf*, vol. 5.

Lieberman, S. and F. J. Miller (eds), *Roman Drama*, New York, Bantam, 1964.

Lovejoy, Arthur O., *The Great Chain of Being*, Cambridge Mass., Harvard University Press, 1961.

Matejka, Ladislav and Irwin R. Titunik (eds), *Semiotics of Art*, Cambridge, MIT Press, 1976.

Moussinac, Leon, *Le Theatre*, Paris, Flammarion, 1966 (Hebrew version – Tel Aviv, Dvir, 1966).

Murrell, John, *Farther West*, Toronto, Coach House Press, 1985.

Ofrat, Gideon, "The Arab in Israeli Drama," *Jerusalem Quarterly* (1979), no. 11.

Noonan, James, Forsyth, Louise, "Drama in French', in William Toye (ed.), *The Oxford Companion to Canadian Literature*, Toronto, Oxford University Press, 1983.

Plant, Richard, and L. W. Conolly, *Drama in English*.

Quigley, Austin, *The Modern Stage and Other Worlds*, New York, Methuen, 1985.

Rokem, Freddie, "Stage, Space and the Fictional World in Modern Theatre," *Aley Sia'ch*, vol. 19/20 (in Hebrew).

Sadan-Loebenstein, Nili, *A. B. Yehoshua: A Monograph*, Tel Aviv, Sifriat Poalim, 1981.

Sartre, Jean Paul, "Les peintures de Giacometti" (*Situations*), Tel Aviv, Hakibbutz Hameuchad, 1984 (in Hebrew).

Schmid, Herta, *Strukturalistische Dramentheorie*, Kronberg TS., Scriptor, 1973 (Skripten Literaturwissenschaft, 3).

Silk, Denis, *Retrievements*, Jerusalem, Keter, 1969.

Skelton, Robin, *The Writings of J. M. Synge*, London, Thames and Hudson, 1971.

Synge, John Millington, *Riders to the Sea*, in John Hampden (ed.), *Twenty One-Act Plays*, London, Dent, 1941.

Sontag, Susan, *Illness as Metaphor*, New York, Vintage Books, 1978.

Toye, William, *The Oxford Companion to Canadian Literature*, Toronto University Press, Oxford, 1983.

Turner, Victor, *From Ritual to Theatre*, New York, Performing Arts Journal Publications, 1982.

Thompson, Judith, an interview with Sandra Tomc, in *Canadian Theatre Review* (1989), no. 59.

Ubersfeld, Anne, "The Space of Phedre," in *Poetics Today* (1980), vol. 2.

Wallace, Robert, "Writing the Land Alive," in Anton Wagner (ed.), *Contemporary Canadian Theatre*, Toronto, Simon & Pierre, 1985.

Wittgenstein, Ludwig, *Tractatus Logico-Philosophicus*, London, Routledge & Kegan Paul, 1960.

Worth, Katherine, "Space and Sound in Beckett's Theatre," in K. Worth (ed.), *Beckett the Shape Changer*, London, Routledge and Kegan Paul, 1975.

Index

Major fictional characters are indexed directly under their names with the story or play in which they figure in brackets after the name.